HEINRICH BÖLL

MODERN GERMAN AUTHORS
New Series

EDITED BY R. W. LAST

VOLUME ONE

HEINRICH BÖLL

WITHDRAWAL AND RE-EMERGENCE

by

JAMES HENDERSON REID

OSWALD WOLFF
London

MODERN GERMAN AUTHORS—New Series
ed. R. W. Last

Volume One: HEINRICH BÖLL—Withdrawal and
Re-emergence

ISBN Cloth 0 85496 047 3
Paper 0 85496 048 1

© 1973 Oswald Wolff (Publishers) Limited,
London W1M 6DR

MADE AND PRINTED IN GREAT BRITAIN BY
THE GARDEN CITY PRESS LIMITED
LETCHWORTH HERTFORDSHIRE
SG6 1JS

CONTENTS

For
Ingrid

NOTE

Except where indicated the translations from the German are by the author. This is also the case with the titles of Böll's works. Titles of the official translations of Böll's works are sometimes misleading; they can be found in the third section of the Select Bibliography.

THE STATE AND THE
ALTERNATIVE SOCIETY

When in October 1972 Heinrich Böll was awarded the
Nobel prize for literature, the response of the conservative Springer press was curious. Apart from Hermann
Hesse in 1946, who had by then been a naturalised Swiss
for twenty-five years, Böll was the first German to be
honoured in this way since Thomas Mann in 1929. Some
justified national pride might have been expected—
Germany was not being internationally remembered for
Nazi atrocities but for post-war achievements. Instead
reactions ranged from the muted, mainly factual report
of *Bild* to the resentful polemic of *Die Welt*, whose
H. Joachim Maitre sought in a lengthy article to dem-
onstrate (*a*) that the Nobel prize usually went to minor
writers, (*b*) that it was a political, often left-wing award,
and (*c*) that both these categories applied to Böll.[1] Böll
had been under consideration for some years. But
already in 1961 *Der Spiegel* reported that the initiatives
for proposing him to the Nobel Prize Committee came
not from Germany but from Sweden.[2] *Bild* claims that of
world-wide sales of 3,500,000 copies of Böll's books, two
million were in the Soviet Union alone. A prophet is not
without honour save in his own country, one might
deduce. In fact *Bild*'s statistics are, as usual, misleading :
they disregard pocket-book editions, and sales of these

9

alone in West Germany are greater than total sales elsewhere.

The immediate cause of Böll's unpopularity on the right was an article which Böll had written earlier in the year for *Der Spiegel* at the height of public hysteria over the urban guerrillas led by Andreas Baader and Ulrike Meinhof. The Baader-Meinhof group had committed arson, murder and a number of armed robberies; they had also issued a manifesto declaring war on West German society. Their effect on the public was quite out of proportion to their actual deeds, but the right-wing press, notably *Bild*, alleged their responsibility for every robbery with violence that took place during their activities. Böll, alarmed at the hysteria and fearing an outbreak of lynch-justice, pleaded for understanding, a cooler atmosphere and a fair trial, appealed to the gang to give themselves up, and attacked *Bild*'s methods of reporting. The storm which followed was unparalleled in post-war German history. The mildest reproach made was that Böll was trivialising the anarchists; many right-wing commentators went further and suggested that he was secretly in favour of both their aims and their methods.[3]

Since 1945 an important feature of the German literary scene has been the tendency of writers to adopt a political—often party-political—stance and for their books to be read in political terms. In 1961, for example, leftist writers, among them Böll, had been attacked in *Die Welt* for their silence over the Berlin wall.[4] Böll's difficulties with the right-wing press can be seen as the culmination of a process of alienation between writers and the CDU-orientated establishment. Two stages in this process can be distinguished. In the 1950's writers were the conscience of the nation, reminding their readers of the atrocities of the immediate past and protesting against a contemporary pursuit of purely material wealth regardless of the values of justice and humanity. In a time of reconstruction and consolidation with the CDU under Adenauer firmly in control these writers posed no serious threat to the government; they were merely, in the memorable expression of Ludwig Erhard, 'Pinscher', terriers snapping at the heels of their masters. However, by the early 1960's, when Erhard used this expression, the situation had changed. Uninterrupted power since 1948 had not been good for the CDU. Adenauer's machinations over the Presidency of the Federal Republic in 1959 had weakened his moral standing; the *Spiegel* affair of 1962 suggested that the CDU had little care for the freedom of the press. A minor economic recession in the mid-1960s and the inadequacy of the government's educational investment policy, which became apparent in student unrest about the same time, brought the Social Democrats to power, first as partner with the CDU in the Grand Coalition of 1966, later in coalition with the Free Democrats in 1969. In this process writers had played their part. In 1961 Martin Walser brought out a collection of essays by various hands on the necessity of a change in government. Since 1965 Günter Grass has been tirelessly and at some cost to his writing campaigning for the SPD. Böll believes that writers have had a considerable effect on the course of German politics since the war, especially among Roman Catholics (AKR, p. 503).[5]

With this background in mind, it is worth first examining in some detail Böll's political outlook, his attitude to the state and to society. As he has become more famous he has become more exposed, requested and willing to sign protest telegrams and to be interviewed on issues of the day. He was, for example, prominent in the campaign against the Emergency Laws passed by the Grand Coalition in 1968, laws which it was felt resembled those by which Hitler came legally to power in 1933 and which might lead to abuse. When the student leader Rudi Dutschke was the victim of an assassination attempt in the same year, Böll with thirteen others, mainly prominent academics including Theodor W. Adorno, Alexander Mitscherlich and Golo Mann, signed a declaration expressing solidarity with the students and denouncing the right-wing press for creating the hysterical atmosphere which had provoked the deed. He has also publicly protested against the Soviet occupation of Czechoslovakia and the inhuman treatment of the Russian intellectuals, especially Solzhenitzyn. Since 1971 he has been President of the International PEN Club and his activities in this area have intensified.

Böll's political standpoint has from earliest times been formed not by theory, reading political writers, but by experience. His 'socialism', if it may be called that, is emotional rather than political. Family influences were favourable to the development of a social conscience. Böll was not shielded from the hunger, unemployment and inflation of his early years, nor did the Church's inactivity in the social sphere go unnoticed. The anti-Nazi stance was inculcated from the start and for Böll there was never any doubt that the result of 1933 would be 1945 (Arnold, p. 9). Nevertheless he did not join any internal resistance movement, nor did he emigrate. He avoided the Hitler Youth Movement, but his dissociation from Hitler's war is best seen in the rather negative fact that he served throughout without advancing beyond the rank of corporal. The war confirmed his hatred of Nazism and installed in him a lasting aversion to military service and all that goes with it, uniforms and decorations. His resistance to West German rearmament and his distrust of the Bundeswehr are prominent motifs of his works. With the writer's eye for significant detail he has pointed out the absurdity of allowing officers to wear their war decorations—but with the swastika omitted.

One feature of his war-time experiences, however, was his first encounter with Marxism through former Communists from Berlin and a friend who taught him the rudiments of dialectical materialism (Arnold, pp. 9–10). Böll is not a Marxist, although he has written sympathetically on Marx. He accepts Marx's description of capitalist society : man is not what he is, but what he possesses. Since Marx's day the individual has been degraded still further to the rank of consumer; not religion but 'expenditure' is now the opium of the people (AKR, p. 86). But Böll's stance is fundamentally anti-materialist. He has described himself as a 'Communist manqué', prevented from becoming one by Hitler on the one hand and Stalin on the other (AKR, p. 504). In 1967 he still believed that Communism offered a hope for mankind. The internal development of Soviet Russia, the persecution of writers particularly, has made him more pessimistic about that country. In 1971, after the successive failures of Czechoslovakia and Cuba he was pinning his hopes on Allende in Chile (Arnold, p. 50).

Böll has generally refused to align himself with any movement and for this he has been attacked from all the stools he has avoided. In 1962 he attacked the SPD for betraying all that it had stood for in the past; the

Godesberg programme of 1959 abandoned all plans for nationalisation (AKR, pp. 125–6). The Grand Coalition seemed to be the final blow, when the SPD helped to form a government under Kiesinger, a former Nazi.[6] By 1971, however, he was expressing support for Willy Brandt (Arnold, pp. 41–2) and in 1972 for the first time he took part in an electoral campaign, making speeches for the SPD as one of the prominent 'citizens for Brandt.'

One specific and illuminating issue to which Böll returns again and again is that of the Currency Reform of 1948. This deceptively simple measure carried out by the Allies in conjunction with the West German authorities laid the basis for economic developments in the 1950's. On 20 June 1948 all the money circulating in the Western territories was declared invalid; on the same day every individual had the right to receive the sum of 40 DM at official centres. Debts and savings were devalued by 90 per cent. The measure looks egalitarian, until one realises that property was not affected; besides, news of the impending event leaked out to the lucky few well in advance, so that on the day itself the shops were suddenly full of goods and fortunes were made overnight. Once again the small savers were ruined, as in 1923. For Heinrich Fähmel in Böll's novel *Billard um halbzehn* (Billiards at half-past nine) (1959) 1948 was simply the confirmation of the 'swindle' perpetrated twenty-five years earlier. In an essay of 1960 Böll divides post-war German history into the periods before and after the Currency Reform: 20 June 1948 was the day when the term 'collective guilt' became meaningful (EHA, p. 437). For writers of Böll's generation a certain nostalgia can be felt in their attitude to the years 1945–8.

For it was a period when, in spite of all the distress and discomfort, there was hope that a new and more just society could be established. The CDU's first manifesto, the Ahlen Programme of 1947, included the demand for nationalisation of coal-mining and monopoly industries. Even the black market had its code of honour and could afford to show generosity to the poor or to children. The short story *Geschäft ist Geschäft* (Business is Business) (1950) tells of a black marketeer who has 'gone straight' and refuses now to give a little girl a lollipop. There were important discussions between Catholics and Communists aimed at reconciling their standpoints.[7] But, as Böll puts it, the Currency Reform merely continued the old game, new counters were distributed and nothing was changed.[8] The Cold War began, the division between the capitalist West and the Communist East was sealed, each part of Germany became an essential factor in the power bloc to which it belonged, rearmament took place, the opportunity was finally lost.

The Currency Reform is a basic symptom of the 'Restoration' which was the main object of Böll's criticism in the 1950's. There were two sides to his attack. On the one hand the prominence given in his work to the past, to the war and its results is intended as a reminder to his compatriots, who have conveniently forgotten Hitler and the Nazi atrocities. On the other he protests at their actively reinstating people and institutions which he feels have been discredited by their association with and abuse by the Nazis. German rearmament is particularly bitterly attacked. Again the early post-war years are praised : true authority for Böll can only be based on a state of absolute external powerlessness.[9] The short satire *Hauptstädtisches Journal*

(Capital Diary) (1957) is the most direct expression of his feelings, but the antimilitarist theme recurs frequently in the later novels. Stories like *Über die Brücke* (Across the Bridge) (1950) and *Nicht nur zur Weihnachtszeit* (Not only at Christmas) (1953) satirise the Restoration in more general terms. In the former we see that wars may come and go and bridges may grow rickety, but nothing will prevent the German housewife from carrying out her window-cleaning schedule. *Nicht nur zur Weihnachtszeit*, possibly Böll's most telling satire, takes the traditional German Christmas as its topic. Aunt Milla insists that everything shall be as it was before the war. At great expense and trouble the necessary paraphernalia are procured: the tree and the tinsel, the clockwork dwarfs and the angel calling 'Peace'. Unfortunately something goes wrong with the works—of Aunt Milla, who now insists on Christmas being celebrated every day of the year, a Restoration in permanence. The most grandiose symbol used by Böll in this connection, however, is St Anthony's Abbey in *Billard um halbzehn*: built by Heinrich Fähmel at the beginning of the century, destroyed by his son Robert at the close of the Second World War, and rebuilt, 'restored' in every detail with the help of Robert's son Joseph in 1958, it is destroyed once more, but only in effigy, at the end of the novel.

In 1952 Böll wrote: 'It is our task to point out that man does not exist to be administered—and that the ravages done to our world are neither merely external nor so trivial that we can presume to heal them in a few short years' (EHA, p. 343). The earlier part of this sentence, the theme of the administration, bureaucracy, is the least specifically German theme in his works. It is also the most basic theme of all, underlying every other. Böll's world is largely divided into two groups of people, those who administer and those who are administered, the 'bureaucrats' in the widest possible sense and those who are trying to preserve some semblance of individuality. In a recent interview Böll spoke of the necessity of protecting the individual from the computer world: 'I see the mechanisation of the world as a form of fascism, as a continuation of fascism.' (Arnold, p. 56). This identification of bureaucracy with fascism establishes the continuity of Böll's attack on historical Nazism and contemporary social processes. In the early stories bureaucracy frequently takes the form of the railway administration. On the level of whimsy, *An der Angel* (On the Hook) (1950) tells of a man who believes that the personnel of a large railway station are mainly occupied with thwarting his attempts to meet his girl-friend. A direct equation of administration and fascism comes in *Der Zug war pünktlich* (The Train was on Time) (1949): the 'sonorous voices' which announce train arrivals and departures through the loudspeakers are the same voices which send people to the front or to concentration camps. Böll's own experience of the war, the helplessness of the individual transported vast distances by a faceless administration, produced this symbol. But the army itself is viewed as one huge bureaucratic machine, both in this story and in the much later *Ende einer Dienstfahrt* (End of an Official Journey) (1966). In *Wo warst du, Adam?* (Where were you, Adam?) (1951), the soldiers who come to fetch Feinhals when he is waiting for Ilona are the 'administrators of death'. Bureaucracy can also appear as the school administration—in *Haus ohne Hüter* (House without

Guardians) (1954) school is the place where resistance is to be broken.

But Böll's attack on bureaucracy takes more subtle forms. His villains are never the front-line criminals but the people in the background, the 'Schreibtischmörder', the opportunists, the men who are as good democrats under one administration as they were Nazis in the other, who therefore lack identity and cannot be brought to justice. Even Filskeit, the commandant of an extermination camp for Jews in *Wo warst du, Adam?* has never been able to kill anyone himself. In *Haus ohne Hüter*, Gäseler, the officer who sent Nella's husband to his death on a senseless mission and on whom she has built a great edifice of hatred, turns out to be merely trivial and boring; the only possible gesture of punishment is a box on the ears from Grandmother.

Gäseler turns up at a literary congress under the auspices of the Catholic Church. Here we find the other two ways in which bureaucracy appears in Böll's works: 'Kultur' and 'Kirche'. Böll is a Roman Catholic and a successful writer: an important part of his world has been on the one hand the Church authorities and administrative organs, and on the other the circus of hangers-on, the parasites, the culture-vultures, the writers of books and learned articles who quickly surround the successful author.

Böll is not a Catholic writer in the sense that Claudel and Mauriac in France were Catholic writers. Theological questions play no greater role in his works than in the works of other, non-Catholic writers. His theological standpoint is in fact probably surprisingly conservative. He seems to reject the more progressive theologians—because they have become alienated from the simple straightforward beliefs of ordinary people, because instead of 'feeding His sheep' (*Billard um halbzehn*) they have become part of the bureaucratic machine. Böll insists again and again that he is a writer who also happens to be a Roman Catholic. The furthest he is prepared to go in determining the relation between the two is reminiscent of Luther's definition of the Christian stable boy—who makes as good a job of cleaning the stables as he can, because he is a Christian; Böll's Christianity as a writer consists in being technically as good as he can (AKR, p. 44). Otherwise his Catholicism as far as the public is concerned, is a question of his tax returns—or was up to 1969, for since that year he has been carrying on a private feud with the Church authorities, refusing to pay his Church taxes as a protest against the Church's identification with the State and order to provoke it into showing that it is prepared to resort to force in order to protect its material interests.[10]

Böll views the Church as a 'bureaucracy' and sees this as a cause of corruption. Bureaucrats, whether Catholic or Communist, are of necessity cushioned against life, estranged from the world of ordinary people, concerned merely with preserving the status quo which they are paid to administer (Arnold, pp. 24–5). And throughout his life the Church as an institution has failed to meet the challenge of every new situation. In the early 1930's it failed to make common cause with the unemployed and the hungry (Arnold, p. 21). The Vatican was the first state to recognise Hitler (EHA, p. 388). After the war the Church was equally quick to identify itself with the economic system on which the Federal Republic was founded (Arnold, p. 22). When West German rearmament was debated, the Church's only reaction was to make plans for a prayer book for Catholic soldiers which would stand up to heavy wear (EHA, p. 390)! When the CDU government proposed to tackle poverty by encouraging everybody to buy property and industrial shares, there was no lack of prelates to proclaim the importance of material goods (AKR, pp. 110–12 and pp. 329–35). From *Und sagte kein einziges Wort* (And he never said a mumbling word) (1953) to *Ansichten eines Clowns* (Views of a Clown) (1963) Böll's attack on bureaucracy was directed mainly at the Roman Catholic Church. More recently the radio plays *Hausfriedensbruch* (Trespass) (1969) and *Aussatz* (Leprosy) (1970) have taken a similar line.

But the Church has not only been safeguarding its own material position. It has also been occupied with aesthetic problems divorced from ethics and the needs of individual humanity. 'For centuries German Catholics have had hardly any concerns other than the perfection of the liturgy and the raising of standards of taste.' (EHA, p. 389). The Church is linked to the aesthetes, the other target of Böll's polemics. As one who has been awarded more literary prizes than any other writer in Germany, possibly in the world, Böll has frequently found himself in the embarrassing position of being lauded by the very circles his books attack. On one such occasion, in Wuppertal in 1958, he adopted Gottfried Benn's distinction between the 'Kunstträger', the artist, and the 'Kulturträger', the aesthete. Ultimately there can be no comprehension between them.[11] The aesthete is another version of Böll's administrator and a common butt of satire: Filskeit, the music lover and Jew exterminator of *Wo warst du, Adam?*, Bur-Malottke of *Doktor*

Murkes gesammeltes Schweigen (Dr. Murke's Collection of Silences) (1955), with his Vicar of Bray-like conversion or deconversion at the appropriate historical moment, who has his counterparts in several characters of *Haus ohne Hüter* and *Ansichten eines Clowns*. These are individual examples of opportunists. But Böll's portrayal of post-war Germany is in some respects that of a totalitarian state, in which the writer is muzzled not by force but by freedom itself, the total freedom of expression which elevates his art into a non-committal aesthetic sphere, where there is only one crime, that of offending against good taste, where form is everything and content rendered sterile and ineffective. An essay of 1961 sees Böll caught 'between prison and museum', whereby East Germany is the prison and West Germany the museum (*Hierzulande*, pp. 53–60). This problem is discussed most fully in the two artist novels *Ansichten eines Clowns* and *Ende einer Dienstfahrt* and will be examined later. At this point it need only be said that the aesthete is the administrator of art, responsible for pigeon-holing it, defusing the bombs in its message, adapting it to the needs of conformist society. Hence Dr. Murke's attempt to infiltrate the sterile tastefulness of Broadcasting House with some *Kitsch*. Another speech at Wuppertal caused a scandal with its demand that art should always 'go too far' in order to test the extent of its so-called freedom. Freedom, says Böll, is meaningless unless it is always being exploited to its limits (AKR, pp. 488–93).

So far we have been describing the object of Böll's criticism. What forces does he set up as alternatives to bureaucratic, conformist, materialist, reactionary, amorphous society? Sometimes he seems to see no hope. His most bitter work to date, *Entfernung von der Truppe*

(Absent without Leave) (1964), openly advises 'desertion', i.e. emigration. The earlier *Nicht nur zur Weihnachtszeit* showed three forms of revolt against the Restoration : one member of the family joins the Communist party, one emigrates, one enters a monastery. Böll may be a 'Communist manqué', but Communism has no chance in West Germany at present. He has not yet emigrated, although he has frequently threatened to do so. The monastery, however, is more immediately significant, if we view it symbolically. In reply to an interviewer's question in 1971 on the possibility of an 'alternative society', Böll replied : 'I believe one is necessary, absolutely necessary, and probably the only possibility for man to protect himself from fascism, automation, the world of the computer' (Arnold, p. 56). Just as in the Dark Ages the monasteries were the repositories of civilisation in the midst of a barbaric world, so we find in Böll's works up to about 1960 the tendency of a withdrawal into a private anti-world. And just as the monasteries later took the offensive to re-establish civilisation in the outside world, so Böll's later works imply some first tentative steps towards a counter-attack.

Before we go on to discuss this development in detail, one prominent feature of Böll's earlier stories is worth examining for the light it sheds on the question of the alternative society. This is the motif of the bizarre profession. The narrator of *Der Mann mit den Messern* (The Man with the Knives) (1948) is taken into the employment of a knife-thrower in a circus; he is the man at whom the knives are thrown. *An der Brücke* (At the Bridge) (1949)[12] tells of a man who works for a statistical office counting the people who cross the bridge. *Der Lacher* (The Laugher) (1952) is about a professional claqueur whose laughter is used for recordings, radio-effects and to spark off laughter at third-rate comedians' jokes. *Bekenntnis eines Hundefängers* (Confession of a Dog-Catcher) (1953) describes a man who goes about looking for unregistered dogs. The narrator of *Hier ist Tibten* (This is Tibten) (1953) is a loudspeaker announcer in a railway station who holds two doctorates, that of *Es wird etwas geschehen* (Something will Happen) (1954) leaves his job at a soap-factory to become the counterpart of the 'Laugher', a professional mourner. *Der Wegwerfer* (The Discarder) (1957) is about a man who saves other people's time by sorting out their mail and throwing away 'bumph'; he is now on the point of branching out to become an 'unpacker' in a large store, where he will save customers the trouble of unpacking the goods they buy.

There are of course 'normal' professions in Böll's works and it is against these that the significance of the 'abnormal' ones can best be gauged. The industrialists are associated with the evils of a political ideology. Martin's grandfather's jam factory in *Haus ohne Hüter* always made its greatest profits during wars, the Schniers of *Ansichten eines Clowns* made their fortune literally from the 'sacred German soil', namely by coal-mining. But the most interesting professions are those mentioned in *Die schwarzen Schafe* (The Black Sheep) (1951) and *Und sagte kein einziges Wort*. The former tells of Uncle Otto, the black sheep of the family, a charming man, particularly good with children, informative on every facet of life, but refusing to take up a regular job. His nephew follows in his footsteps. Like his uncle, he is full of plans—in a single afternoon he contemplates becoming a painter, gardener, mechanic and sailor—but realises none. Fred Bogner of *Und sagte kein einziges Wort* changes his job every three years, because he cannot take any occupation seriously. The two stories illuminate each other. Like Fred, the black sheep is an outsider who refuses to respect the social conventions. Once indeed he did take a job—in a factory which made impossibly trashy furniture. Fred's current position in the telephone exchange of the Church's Central Offices is one which gives him insight into the empty activity of the bureaucratic machine.

The bizarre professions have a similar function: they reveal the hollowness of society. The knife-thrower's assistant is taking part in an act to give the audience a thrill; they must feel that blood might flow—this only three years after the end of the war. It is a society in which not even the primitive reactions of laughter and sadness are spontaneous any longer, one in which the wrappings have become more important than the contents, and the individual is being reduced to an item in a statistician's table—not even the dogs are exempt from registration. However, the central characters of all these stories have succeeded in carving out for themselves a position in which their individuality is relatively secured. The knife-thrower's assistant tells us that he has at last found an occupation which permits him to forget the world and dream. In this he resembles the narrator of *Es wird etwas geschehen*: in a professional mourner meditation and indolence are desirable and a duty. In contrast to Wunsiedel's soap-factory with its hectic atmosphere, this occupation leaves room for the inner life. So too with the man at the bridge: by refusing to count a girl who crosses the bridge regularly, he is preserving *his* independence from statistics. The station-announcer of *Hier ist Tibten* alone knows that the relics of a Roman child admired by thousands of tourists every year are fakes. The dog-catcher too admits to making individual exceptions from time to time—in fact his own dog is unregistered—and so preserves his individual freedom.

Thus all of them have found a way of preserving some semblance of private life untouched by bureaucracy. Unlike Fred Bogner, they are all outwardly respectable citizens, although more or less uneasily so; and many of them are apprehensive that someone might one day ask them what they do for a living. But their revolt, if there is one, is sterile. The census man reports that his superiors make allowances for errors. Not even Dr. Murke achieves more than the transient satisfaction of making Bur-Malottke decline the phrase 'that higher being whom we honour' through all its cases, and his collection of silences belongs to a completely private world. Society is quite unaffected. The chapters which follow will trace the development of this theme from the pure individualism and passive resistance of Böll's earlier works to the search for a more militant counterculture or alternative society in his more recent ones. We shall be concerned mainly with the novels, whose structures illuminate this theme in a most striking way.[13]

2

WAR

Böll's first publication was a short story, *Die Botschaft* (The Message), which appeared in 1947. It tells of a soldier who has the duty of visiting his friend's wife after the war to tell her of her husband's death and to bring her his personal belongings. On arrival at the house he discovers that she is living with another man. When she is given her husband's wedding-ring, watch and paybook she bursts into tears: 'Memory seemed to pierce her with swords. At that moment I realised that the war would never be over, never, as long as somewhere a wound was still bleeding which it had inflicted.' This fundamental credo must be remembered in taking into account the role played by the war in Böll's works. The war has shaped modern Germany, politically and socially, although the Germans would like to forget it. Böll is the man who cannot forget it. His novels consistently describe contemporary events: the date of writing and the date of the action described in them correspond more or less exactly. But even twenty-five years later the characters of *Gruppenbild mit Dame* (Group Portrait with Lady) (1971) come back again and again to this basic experience.

Böll's early works, *Der Zug war pünktlich*, *Wo warst du, Adam?* and eleven of the stories of *Wanderer, kommst du nach Spa...* ('Traveller, if you come to

Spa . . .) (1950) deal with the war directly. The German writer of war stories is obviously in a different position from that of his English or American counterpart. The latter have a clear tradition in which to write, what one might call the fairy-tale tradition, in which there are clear-cut issues, heroes and villains on a personal level and the triumph of good (i.e. our men) over evil (i.e. the others). There is in fact no lack of German war novels. Hans Helmut Kirst, who has had possibly the greatest commercial success abroad of all German writers, made his reputation in this mode. One way of avoiding the difficulty is to choose that part of the war in which the German armies were being victorious; this Böll never does—all of his war stories are set after Stalingrad. More frequent is the avoidance of the political or moral issues in order to concentrate on personal conflicts behind the lines, spicing these where possible with pornography or near-pornography, as in recent works by Hildegard Gartmann (*Blitzmädchen*) and Hans Lebert (*Der Feuerkreis*). The relation between sex, violence and pornography is a complex one; it is curious that not even Böll can refrain from introducing an attempted rape into the scene in *Wo warst du, Adam?* in which the Jews are brutally murdered.

A war novel is a kind of historical novel and the historical novel will usually try to interpret history by putting events into a meaningful pattern. The keynote of Böll's experience of the war, however, was its 'meaninglessness' (EHA, p. 385). Perhaps the most respectable conservative writer on the subject of war is Ernst Jünger, and in view of the scorn with which Jünger is mentioned in *Als der Krieg zu Ende war* (When the War was Over) (1962) it is worth comparing Böll's attitude with that of

Jünger. In *Der Kampf als inneres Erlebnis* (1922) Jünger
praises war as a 'natural law' similar to the sexual
instinct, an experience in which the natural impulses
which society has repressed come into their own again.
Even during the Second World War Jünger was able
to mythologise war in terms of the mystical bond which
unites the opposing camps.[14]

For Böll, however, as for Saint-Exupéry, whom he
quotes in one of the epigraphs to *Wo warst du, Adam?*,
war is a disease. It is something which happens to one,
not something in which one actively engages. Böll always
associates tedium with war. For Jünger too boredom
was always a danger,[15] but one which he invariably
overcame—in nature study, in intellectual discussions,
in combat. There are few descriptions of actual engage-
ments with the enemy in Böll's works. The characteristic
situation is that of the soldier waiting for the war to
come to him or for himself to be sent into action. Location is interesting in this respect. *Der Zug war pünktlich*
has three main locations: a train, a restaurant and a
brothel. *Wo warst du, Adam?* is set mainly in hospitals
or pubs. Passivity is the keynote throughout. When
incidents are described, the individual soldier is baffled
by them. In *Wo warst du, Adam?* Feinhals is twice sent
into battle: but the war remains either a noise or a
meaningless manoeuvre of hide-and-seek with the enemy.
Böll does not believe in heroes (AKR, pp. 477–80); at
best his individuals are part of a team, a collective.
But even the comradeship which this implies and which
is a traditional motif of war literature is singularly lacking in Böll's works. The opening scene of *Wo warst du,
Adam?* includes the unforgettable description of a
company of soldiers struggling with one another to get

their tin mugs under a single water tap. The individual soldier is seldom in the same place for long enough for deeper personal relationships to develop. In any case, death may intervene at any moment—the narrator of *Als der Krieg ausbrach* (When the War Began) (1962) loses his friend in the first action of the war. Andreas in *Der Zug war pünktlich* remains from start to finish imprisoned in his own self. In the course of the story he meets three people, two soldiers and Olina, a prostitute. The soldiers relate in turn their personal experiences and feelings but Andreas merely listens, dreams of the past, tries to pray. Conversations, dialogues do not develop.[16] Only at the very end is he released from the prison of his self, talks to Olina—and shortly afterwards is killed. *Wiedersehen in der Allee* (Reunion in the Avenue) (1948) describes an apparently happy friendship between the narrator and Hecker, who are alone together for long periods in the trenches. But their comradeship exists largely without words—shortly before he dies Hecker realises that he has always done the talking, the other has merely listened. In *Aufenthalt in X* (Sojourn in X) (1950) the narrator's loneliness is emphasised. A chance encounter with a drunken comrade whom he prevents from shooting an officer, ends with a visit to a pub. The drunkard is loquacious, the narrator says nothing. The three young soldiers of *Damals in Odessa* (That Time in Odessa) (1950) have exhausted their news and have nothing more to say to one another. In *Wo warst du, Adam?* Feinhals has no comrades. Most of the people he meets are not likable, but even on the occasions when friendship might have developed he remains silent. When he visits Finck's family at the end of the war he cannot bring himself to tell them how their son met his death—

29

clutching a case of Tokay wine which his commanding officer had ordered. The catastrophe is too great to be encompassed in words. More significantly still, when Lieutenant Brecht tries to draw him out on the subject of the war, he remains non-committal. One reason for the breakdown in communication and personal relationships is the totalitarian state in which they live—it is safer to keep one's mouth shut. Accordingly monologues and inner monologues are an important feature of Böll's narrative technique.

War for Böll is meaningless. It would have meaning if it were shown to foster personal relationships or the virtues of heroism and self-sacrifice. But it does not. Schmitz and Schröder are potential heroes in *Wo warst du, Adam?*, remaining at their posts to tend the wounded as the Russians advance. But they die because of their own lethargy: when Schröder goes out towards the Russians bearing the white flag he steps on an unexploded shell which he ought to have removed weeks before, the Russians think themselves under attack and destroy the hospital.

In another sense war would be given meaning if it were related in some way to an underlying ideology, if, for example, the causes of the war were shown or if it were interpreted as the necessary concomitant of capitalism, as Brecht implies in *Mutter Courage* (Mother Courage). Böll makes no attempt to do this. His stories are told from a limited point of view. The vast majority of the short stories are first person narratives. The remainder are told from the point of view of one or more individual characters. With one brief exception, which will be examined in due course, the external, commenting, 'omniscient' narrator is not found. Moreover, this limited point of view is never that of somebody who might be expected to have insight into causes and connections, but almost invariably that of the non-political, mediocre 'little man'. Bressen and Filskeit, the 'villains' of *Wo warst du, Adam?*, give us some insights into the Nazi mentality and through the former we learn of certain parallels between the army bureaucracy and that of society in the wider sense. But only indirectly and by implication. There is no critical perspective. Böll's works have been well received in the Communist world. But on this point he is criticised again and again. It is partly a question of political ideology, partly it belongs to the long and complex argument on the question of realism which has been going on between West and East since the 1930's.[17]

In yet another sense, merely to write about war in artistic form is to give it meaning, arranging it into a pattern of events, describing it as a coherent whole with a beginning and ending or in terms of the biography of an individual soldier. Böll attacks this problem in an interesting way. The short story is his favourite form (Bienek, p. 140). The point about the short story is that it does not recount events in coherent succession like the *Novelle* or the novel; it does not have a plot. Instead it illuminates, by concentrating on a single moment, a unique event, an encounter with life. *Wanderer, kommst du nach Spa...*, for example, describes a soldier's return, badly wounded, to the school which he left a few weeks earlier and which now has become a temporary hospital. On the blackboard is still the beginning of the text from the monument to the heroes of Thermopylae which he had begun to write and had to break off for lack of space. The truncated text reflects the mutilated narrator, mutilated by a war waged in abuse of the ideology of the text itself. No development is shown, no plot, merely a juxtaposition of actuality and ideology.

Der Zug war pünktlich was Böll's first independent publication. Preceded by some ten short stories, some of which, for example *An der Brücke*, are undoubtedly superior, its length may have been its undoing. It falls into two clear halves, the first describing a train journey back to the front, the second Andreas's experiences in a brothel, his attempt to desert and his death in an ambush. The strength of the work lies in its description of the train journey across Germany and occupied Poland : the station platforms at night time with the tired girls serving coffee, the grime of the train, the soldiers sleeping in the corridor, playing cards or singing their interminable songs. The passivity and absurdity of the soldier's existence are well captured. But the second half introduces the impossibly melodramatic and sentimental story of Olina, a Polish prostitute who originally wished to study music, and now works for the resistance network gathering strategic information from her customers. She and Andreas fall in love to the music of Beethoven and amid copious tears. Some stylistic weaknesses of the first half—a constant striving for effect by means of imagery —become even worse in the second. There are attempts to contrast or parallel the two halves. The meaningful life of resistance to the oppressors contrasts with the soldier's acceptance of his existence. But there is no suggestion that resistance on the part of the latter would be at all possible. Besides, Andreas finds the brothel administration strongly reminiscent of the army—there are oppressed and oppressors here too.

The story is told from the point of view mainly of

Andreas, later of Andreas and Olina alternately. However, at the end of the first page there is an interpolation by an anonymous, external narrator unparalleled in all Böll's works. As the train leaves Andreas calls out in despair that he is going to die. There follows a long general comment. Sometimes words spoken unthinkingly take on magical qualities, anticipating the future, assuming the mantle of Fate : 'Lovers and soldiers, the doomed and those who are filled with the cosmic force of life are sometimes unexpectedly given this power, they are endowed and burdened with a sudden illumination . . . and the word sinks, sinks into them.' The power of the word remains for Böll an important preoccupation, as many of his critical essays and speeches testify. Totalitarian regimes abuse language for propaganda purposes. Since 1945 certain words have lost currency for Böll completely : 'Duty, fatherland, honour, obedience' (AKR, p. 302). Fascism's contemporary equivalent, the administrative machine, is similarly engaged in debasing language. Advertising and the media are especially guilty (EHA, p. 441). In view of the constant stream of words pouring from the radio *Dr. Murkes gesammeltes Schweigen* regards the only justifiable attitude to language as silence. However, in no other story of Böll's does an anonymous, impersonal narrator come out into the open with such a direct comment. And since he does not do so again in *Der Zug war pünktlich* we are justified in viewing it as a stylistic flaw, due to Böll's artistic immaturity.

Wo warst du, Adam? is free of most of the defects of *Der Zug war pünktlich*. The tone is much more restrained. Events are allowed to speak for themselves without the intervention of a commenting narrator or overdone images. The only jarring notes are the rather operatic deaths of Ilona, mown down by bullets as she sings the litany for All Saints, and of Feinhals, killed by shells from German guns just as he reaches the threshold of his parent's house; simultaneously the white flag of surrender which they had hoisted is hit and falls on him. Böll is much more relaxed in this work and is able to introduce some—grimly—humorous touches, as in the story of the bridge which is destroyed by partisans, re-built by German soldiers just in time for them to have to destroy it again when the Russians approach. Although Ilona's name is an anagram of that of the heroine of the earlier work, she is a much more realistic figure, a Hungarian schoolteacher, a Catholic Jew, first encoun-tered as a face on a school photograph, and with no illusions about the future.

Wo warst du, Adam? covers a longer span of time than Böll's other novels. Most of it takes place in the autumn of 1944, the final chapter in the spring of 1945. But narrative time is really irrelevant. There is no plot, no linear succession of events leading to a climax. The German army is as beaten at the beginning as at the end. There is no central figure. Feinhals is the most important individual but is actually 'on scene' for less than half of the novel. Many commentators have denied that it is a novel at all, but rather a collection of short stories. In this respect too it is a much more satisfactory portrayal of the absurdity of war than *Der Zug war pünktlich* with its rather traditional *Novelle*-like form. But beyond this *Wo warst du, Adam?* has the narrative structure characteristic of all Böll's novels, one that is based not on plot, time and character, but on montage and leitmotivs. It is a montage of several internal points of view.

Occasionally an external narrator can be detected, as at the beginning of Chapter 3, but he is never obtrusive and quickly merges with the point of view of one of the characters.[18] The montage quality of this technique is accentuated by the 'openness' of the beginning of most of the chapters. Thus Chapter 2 begins with the words : 'He heard a voice saying "Bressen" . . .', and it is some time before we realise that the 'he' is not the Feinhals of Chapter 1 but Bressen himself, whom we had previously met briefly as an unnamed colonel. Feinhals appears briefly at the end of this chapter as an anonymous soldier with his arm in a sling—for Bressen does not know him, although the reader does. Feinhals is reduced at this point to the status of a leitmotiv. More obvious leitmotivs are those of illness—war is a 'disease'—and military decorations. Many of the soldiers are ill, from the jaundiced General down to Greck and Finck with their stomach ailments; the others are all incapacitated at one time or other. Böll's contempt for military decorations is well-documented; in this novel he rather overdoes the motif. Other linking devices are colours, frequently important in Böll's works. The red stars on the Russian tanks at the end of Chapter 3 become the 'patches of colour' at the beginning of the next; these resolve themselves as piles of reddish-yellow apricots and green gherkins, which become in Chapters 6 and 7 the red and green furniture vans respectively.

Böll's war stories are utterly pessimistic. The war machine has the individual firmly in its grasp. Prayer is the only possible solution, not prayer for divine intervention, in the hope of reforming the world, but 'in order to console God', as Ilona puts it. Everything else is

doomed to destruction. Feinhals learns not to take anything earthly too seriously. But this insight is followed
at once by death. Solidarity does not arise. Where it
begins to do so it is at once nipped in the bud. Böll's
monastery is at this stage a very lonely, withdrawn
place.

3

THE FAMILY NOVELS OF THE 1950's

Post-war, restorative society is conveyed through the medium of the family. Marriage and the relations between parents and children are the main themes of the novels of the 1950's. Both have become problematic for reasons connected with National Socialism and the War. The disintegration of the family shown in *Nicht nur zur Weihnachtszeit* foreshadows later developments. *Und sagte kein einziges Wort* describes a marriage which has broken down, partly because the war has destroyed the living accommodation which would have made it possible, partly because the partners are unable to keep pace with or conform to contemporary life. *Haus ohne Hüter* examines two families whose heads were killed in the war. *Billard um halbzehn* shows three generations of one family and relates them to the various stages of the social and political development of Germany in the twentieth century.

The loneliness of Böll's protagonists in war has been mentioned. After the war things are little different. Practically all the main characters are widows or widowers. Those whom the war has spared have been separated by nature : in *Haus ohne Hüter* Albert's wife Leen died of appendicitis. But in any case marriage has become ideologically suspect. In *Haus ohne Hüter* Nella is prepared to become Albert's mistress, but not his wife.

She remembers a grotesque incident at the beginning of the war when 5,000 wives came to visit their husbands and 5,000 couples had to be accommodated in barracks, stables, wherever there was room, so that, as she puts it, the school-beginners of seven years later, the cannon-fodder of twenty years later could be conceived. Marriage is a social institution, important for the national economy, it is an aspect of the administration—here in league with the Church, for Pater Willibrord speaks unctuously of marriages made in heaven and prays for the victory of the Führer. The discredit thus heaped on the institution remains in the post-Nazi years. Nella cannot be taken as Böll's mouthpiece, but her attitude corresponds to some aspects of Böll's presentation of marriage elsewhere. In *Ansichten eines Clowns* Schnier refuses to marry Marie, because of the Church's insistence on a written undertaking to have his children brought up as Catholics —marriage is a bureaucratic institution. Walter Fendrich in *Das Brot der frühen Jahre* (The Bread of our Early Years) (1955) rejects materialist society and the Church which has embraced it; in the desert, he says, emergency marriages, that is marriages without a priest, are in order. Böll attacks the Church's distrust of sexuality. He frequently criticises its one-sided identification of morality with sexual morality (e.g. EHA, pp. 379 ff.). Marriage as the mere legalisation of sexuality is inadequate. Even in *Und sagte kein einziges Wort* marriage is problematic. It is not the case, as W. A. Coupe declares, that there is no questioning of the sacrament of marriage in his novel. Nor is it the case that the Bogners' problem is purely an economic one.[19] Käte dreams of a life without marriage. And Fred has left not only because of their impossible living conditions, but because of his restless character, his inability to take seriously any social institution which involves routine and continuity. His frequent change of job has already been mentioned. He is faithful to his wife, but only just. He returns to Käte in the end, not because of the ultimatum she gives him, but because of a chance meeting in the street, when he sees her as it were for the first time. The final chapter of the novel is quite clear. It begins with a description of a normal working day, emphasising the mechanical repetitiveness of everything from the advertisements in the shops down to Fred's own job. Marriage too involves such a routine. Fred notes the 'boredom of marriage' when he visits the Büchlers—who are not even married. And it is only his sudden rediscovery of the uniqueness of his wife and his marriage—they have 'prayed together'—that makes him return home. It is not the sacrament nor the institution of marriage that is upheld, for these have become tainted with the fascism of bureaucracy. Instead we find the search for a community not based on bureaucratic principles, found in this case in the personal relationship of two people who happen also to be married. Fred and Käte have prayed together : as in the war novels it is an inward-facing relationship.

The family unit in the wider sense is equally problematic. To an extent greater than in most countries the German family has been almost an ideology in itself —from 1953 to 1969 there was actually a Federal Cabinet Minister for Families. There are two opposing camps in current sociological thinking on the German family. The conservative school around Helmut Schelsky finds positive values in it : a haven in the superficial bustle of industrial society, a place where the individual can retain his identity, and which Hitler could not penetrate. Against this Rolf Dahrendorf sees the family as a pre-industrial, backward-looking phenomenon, interested in fostering merely private virtues—respectability, tidiness etc.—rather than the public virtues of good citizenship, basically apolitical and therefore potentially anti-democratic.[20] Elements of both attitudes are to be found in Böll's search for an alternative society.

There are very few families in Böll's work which correspond to the intact haven of individuality and resistance to fascism described by Schelsky. The Bogners are just able to maintain their marriage; their family life is non-existent. The war has destroyed the family life of the Bachs and Brielachs of *Haus ohne Hüter*. Martin Bach frequently has to breakfast by himself or finds the house empty when he returns from school, and depends on the housekeeper for solace. His friend Heinrich has from an early age had to run the Brielach household. Walter Fendrich has ceased his regular visits to his father. Hans Schnier lost all respect for his parents when his sister Henriette was sent off to die 'heroically resisting' the invaders at the end of the war.

But Böll goes further. On the face of it *Billard um halbzehn* shows a family which has survived the pressures of political and economic developments. The very name Fähmel suggests the prototype 'family'. Robert is almost a hermit. He never confronts his clients directly, not even by telephone. But he is always available for his family. Nevertheless, the relationship is barely more than a formal one. He dreads being left alone with his father for half an hour; he has never told his children that he helped to destroy the abbey his father built. And the Fähmel family radically changes in the course of the novel; Robert adopts Hugo the hotel boy. As for Brecht in *Der Kaukasische Kreidekreis* (The Caucasian Chalk Circle) the ties of blood are insufficient or irrelevant. For this the Nazis with their ancestry-fixation are at least partly to blame. Robert's brother Otto became a Nazi and a 'stranger'. Marianne, Robert's prospective daughter-in-law, refuses to recognise her mother, whose Nazi ideology made her try to kill Marianne at the end of the war. The 'voice of the blood is a lie', comments Schrella and this is why he refuses to get married. The family unit as such is ideologically suspect and Böll's search for a genuine community must take other paths.

Structurally, the family novels of the 1950's follow the pattern established in *Wo warst du, Adam?* The narrative is related from a number of independent, restricted, internal points of view. The story time is radically limited, but extended into the past by means of flashbacks and memories. The whole is held together by montage and leitmotivs.

Of all Böll's novels *Und sagte kein einziges Wort* received possibly the greatest critical acclaim in its day, and it finally established his reputation. One reason was no doubt its topicality. The Catholic Church was struck on a particularly sensitive nerve. It has considerably dated and is the weakest of the three family novels. In tone there is a return to the hysteria of *Der Zug war pünktlich*, especially in the chapters devoted to Käte. In fact it is the character of Käte which is least bearable. Fred the drifter is much more convincing. Böll is not good at presenting decisive, energetic characters except as caricatures, and Käte is rather reminiscent of the people in Wunsiedel's factory (*Es wird etwas geschehen*). Particularly absurd is her sudden realisation in the midst of some savage scrubbing that it is Sunday and a rest day : earlier, *Über die Brücke* took precisely the German housewife's cleaning programme as the target of its satire.

On the credit side *Und sagte kein einziges Wort* is one of the few German novels to give a vivid picture of city life at a particular historical moment, comparable in a limited way to Alfred Döblin's *Berlin Alexanderplatz*. The time is September 1952, the place recognisably Cologne, although the street names have all been disguised. The city is still full of ruins from the bombing raids. It is a place of snack-bars, unheated churches which have been temporarily repaired, wooden shanty-like shops and cafés. There is an acute housing shortage, although the city has already started to build council flats. The 'Economic Miracle' has begun : the Büchlers are paying for their furniture by instalments and the hardware shop which Fred passes every morning is advertising winter sports. The conference mania has got under way. Both the bustle of the streets and the noise of the over-crowded city tenement in which the Bogners rent their room are vividly captured.

This precisely observed location is of considerable structural importance in the novel. It is conveyed primarily through Fred, who is constantly on the move, first on his tutoring round, later in search of a hotel for Käte and himself, then on his way to work and finally on the errand which leads to the decisive encounter with Käte. She on the other hand is mainly static, at home or with Fred in the hotel. There is then a basic contrast between the peregrinatory Fred and Käte, the pole around which he moves, and it counterpoints their characters : Fred is passive, Käte dynamic. A submerged pattern can be detected in this structure, that of the *Odyssey*.[21] Fred is Odysseus, Käte Penelope. The novel relates Fred's search for his spiritual and material home —the final words are 'nach Hause' (home). The analogy must not be pressed, but is worth making not least in view of the frequent visions in the novel of life as an eternal and inevitable repetition of movements or attitudes.

The Bogners' physical separation is underlined by the narrative point of view. It is a first-person narrative, told by Fred and Käte in alternate chapters. There is no suggestion anywhere that they are collaborating in the story. People whom they meet independently, the café-girl, for example, are described anew as if the reader had not already met them. There is no community of narrative, just as there is no community in their marriage. Nor do we have the impression that they are looking back at past events, in the traditional autobiographical manner. There is no anticipation of a future beyond the events narrated, as there is, for example in *Das Brot der frühen Jahre*, where Fendrich remarks that he has often wondered what would have happened if he had not met Hedwig. *Und sagte kein einziges Wort* consists of two interlocked interior monologues. A leitmotiv is the mirror. The outer appearance of both characters is established when they catch sight of themselves in a mirror. This emphasises their almost narcissistic isolation. However, it is also related to the interior monologue technique, which can convey immediate visual impressions of its subject only in this way. Wilhelm Grenzmann was puzzled by the technique and rather fancifully suggested that the two were keeping a diary.[22] The novel might well have benefited from being told in the third person, as indirect interior monologue, like Böll's other novels. W. A. Coupe's main criticism, that the Bogners are much too articulate to be plausible,[23] might thereby have become groundless.

The events described cover just under forty-eight hours, from midday on a Saturday to shortly before midday on the following Monday. The past living on in the present is shown through Fred's and Käte's memories of it. Leitmotiv patterns are prominent. Accompanying Fred's odyssey through the city are the twin motifs of the Catholic procession and the druggists' conference. The one contains the formal elements of Catholicism which are useless if not actually hostile to the plight of the Bogners; the other represents the purely material, secular attitude—contraception—which they also reject; both are part of the impersonal, administrative world. Closer to Käte is the leitmotiv of the novel's title. It has both Christian and secular implications. The Negro spiritual from which it is taken suggests that Käte's sufferings are parallel to the sufferings of Christ. Fred's mother too used to suffer in silence. The talkative dragon Frau Franke contrasts with her kind-hearted, taciturn husband. The mongol child cannot speak a word, but seems to be in contact with some higher reality. The motif is repeated more light-heartedly in *Doktor Murkes gesammeltes Schweigen*. For one characteristic of bureaucracy which it has in common with National Socialism is its inflationary use of language, whether it be the Bishop's banalities, the permanent radio programme or the advertisement slogans of the druggists. Silence is indeed a mark of the blessed. But once more it points to the inward-lookingness of Böll's position at the time.

Language is an important theme of *Haus ohne Hüter* too. The unrepentant Nazi Gäseler is unmasked when he falls into the 'jargon of earlier times'. Advertising slogans, commercial and religious, are prominent. But it is especially the gulf between the child's and the adult's conception of language that Böll is exploring in this novel, whether he is satirising the banalities of social intercourse or showing how puzzling to children such words are as the obscenity which Frau Brielach said to the baker. The adult world uses language as a camouflage; children are as yet unspoiled by administrative forms.

Haus ohne Hüter was Böll's most ambitious novel so far. Almost twice the length of the previous one, it points forward in many ways to *Billard um halbzehn*: its symbolism, the three-generation family with a grandmother who wishes to assassinate a former Nazi, the third-person narrative told from a complex montage of internal points of view. This last feature again underlines the lack of communication between the characters, especially the adults and the children. It is conceived on a much more generous scale than the earlier works. Apart from the five main characters, several more or less exotic minor characters are introduced : Glum, a refugee from Siberia, Bolda, the Bachs' housekeeper, Martin's grandmother, a formidable old lady with many disconcerting idiosyncrasies. Towards the end one has the feeling that Böll is trying too hard to fill out his novel, particularly when Bresgote, Albert's employer, offers to kill Gäseler and tries to rape Nella. Nella is the least satisfactory of the characters, a *femme fatale* with an irresistible smile. Böll was obviously aware of this and tried to compensate by introducing an element of 'high camp' into the story.

Nella has seen so many bad films that she experiences life itself as a film. 'Did desperadoes always have to be unshaven?' she thinks, as Bresgote advances.

The film is one of the important leitmotivs of *Haus ohne Hüter*. All of the characters are affected. Albert too is frequently plagued by the feeling that he has seen it all before—in a film. The cinema is primarily a symbol of escapism—for Frau Brielach it is a place where one can 'forget'. It is a place of unreality: Nella imagines her life with Rai as a film which was arbitrarily cut. But it is also related to restorative society and the loss of focus on the important things in life. Martin cannot believe what Albert tells him, that the Nazis murdered Absalom Billig: 'Murder happened only in films . . .' And Frau Brielach distrusts the baker when he talks of love: 'Love was something you saw in films . . .' These two poles in Böll's thinking, the atrocities of the past and human love, have both been delegated by contemporary German society to the unreal world of the cinema.

The musical structure of Böll's novels is particularly obvious in this novel. Chapter 1 introduces all the themes and the main leitmotivs. Martin's thoughts in bed touch on all the members of the Bach household, on his father, whom he has never seen, on Gäseler, the 'murderer' of his father, on his friend Heinrich and the difficulties of the Brielach family, on sexuality, on the catechism and its problems, on Bietenhahn, where nobody has problems and where the novel ends. The final chapter echoes the beginning. Martin is once more in bed listening to the sounds outside and thinking about what has happened. There have been developments: Albert has resolved to take him away from the unstable atmosphere of his home, an anticipation of the adoption of Hugo in *Billard um halbzehn*; Frau Brielach has moved to yet another 'husband'; Nella has discovered that Gäseler is merely boring. But it is not certain how permanent any of these developments will be. Böll is mainly describing a situation; solutions are much hazier than in the earlier novels. Much of the narrative is taken up with the rehearsal of what happens regularly. It is therefore difficult to pinpoint the time structure of what development there is. But the characteristic compression of narrative time and expansion into the past can easily be observed. The final twelve chapters all take place on a Friday, the third chapter on the previous Monday or Tuesday.

This pattern of compression and expansion is repeated with regard to location. The action of the novel is confined to Brunn and environs; but by association Böll includes the whole of Europe from Siberia to Ireland. However, unlike *Und sagte kein einziges Wort*, *Haus ohne Hüter* does not depict a specific geographical or historical situation in any detail. The action occurs in September 1953; there are still ruins, but they are not obtrusive. The location is suburban, rather than urban— even rural at the end. The realism of setting in the previous novel gives way to symbolism.

Thus the discovery of rats in the cellar prompts Albert to take Martin away—to the country, away from his feckless mother. The second part of this symbolism is not clear: does Böll see hope in a more genuine rural community? So shortly after the Nazi abuse of a peasant ideology, this is disconcerting. The songs sung by the guests in the village inn evoke further associations with an evil past. The ending is perhaps ironic. Much more successful, even brilliantly so, is the visit to the old casemate in the woods, where Albert and Rai were

47

tortured and Absalom Billig murdered by SA men. It is now being commercially exploited in the cultivation of mushrooms. Nearby Grebhake and Wolters were seen indulging in homosexuality, and it is not difficult to find erotic symbols in the description of the mushroom beds. The casemate is a symbol of the subconscious to which the unpleasant memories of the past have been banished, repressed by the commercial materialism of contemporary society.

Finally there is Vohwinkels Weinstuben, the first-class restaurant where Martin is regularly initiated by his grandmother into good living and where he is equally regularly sick. Hotels and restaurants clearly hold enormous fascination for Böll. *Der Zug war pünktlich* describes an expensive meal in an aristocratic restaurant in Lvov. In *Wo warst du, Adam?* Greck visits a village pub and encounters veiled hostility from the natives, Frau Susan keeps the inn at Berczaba, and several of the characters work in restaurants in civilian life. A café in *Und sagte kein einziges Wort* is the location of what is possibly the most positive incident of the novel. In *Haus ohne Hüter*, besides Vohwinkels Weinstuben, we enter Luigi's ice parlour, a riverside pub frequented by Albert and the village inn kept by his mother in Bietenhahn. In *Das Brot der frühen Jahre* Fendrich makes his break with the past in the Café Joos. Heinrich and Robert Fähmel in *Billard um halbzehn* exercise their eccentricities in the Café Kroner and the Hotel Prinz Heinrich respectively. Böll's characters obviously have little home life! In most cases the restaurant or hotel is a microcosm of society in general. It is a place where the social insignia, like rank insignia in the army, are observed to the letter (Bressen in *Wo warst du, Adam?*), where everything can be regulated by money (Frau Holstege's cheques in *Haus ohne Hüter*), a place which is discreet and allows an individual to set up his private mythology —provided he can pay for it (the Fähmels). It is not always a negative symbol; the poorer and smaller it is, the more likely it is to offer refuge to the outsiders. The provincial eating places in *Ende einer Dienstfahrt* are quite different from Vohwinkels Weinstuben. For the affluent society reflected in the latter has conveniently ignored the poverty and hunger of the Brielachs, the ones who cannot keep up.

Restaurants are also important in view of the sacramental meaning which Böll frequently puts on the acts of eating and drinking. This is increasingly clear from *Das Brot der frühen Jahre* onwards. The central symbol of this work is conveyed by the title. The most basic, primitive food, bread, is set against the more Lucullan delights of the restaurants which have sprung up with Germany's material prosperity. *Billard um halbzehn* is constructed on a whole series of related motifs : in the religious sphere the phrase 'Feed my lambs' and the 'sacrament of the buffalo', in the social sphere the Hotel Prinz Heinrich and the Café Kroner. On Robert's first meeting with Edith 'he realised for the first time what eating really is'; Schrella, her brother, regards it as an 'act of brotherliness'. The act of eating together is communion in both senses of the word. As such it may form the nucleus of an alternative society, although the Establishment is doing its best to pervert this act too.

Billard um halbzehn culminates the development of Böll's narrative technique in the 1950's. The novels which succeed it are all looking for new paths : *Ansichten eines Clowns* restricts its point of view to a single person, *Ende einer Dienstfahrt* is narrated from an external point of view and *Gruppenbild mit Dame* plays with the device of the pseudo-biographer. *Billard um halbzehn* has some ten different internal points of view. The frequent change of perspective within a chapter, and the change within a perspective from direct to indirect interior monologue and from there to direct speech demand some considerable patience from the reader. Even Maurice Boucher, for example, confused Robert and Heinrich Fähmel[24] and the *Times* reviewer of the English translation clearly felt it not worth the trouble.[25] Most puzzling are the chapters devoted to Johanna Fähmel, since she is the inmate of a mental hospital and not all of what she says can be taken at face value. This basic difficulty, however, is not arbitrary. All the members of the Fähmel family are to some extent, like Johanna, prisoners in the 'enchanted castle' of their selves. And it is Schrella, the 'outsider', returning from years of exile, who breaks the spell and releases them.

One important aspect of the 'enchanted castle' is that in it time stands still. Böll, like many twentieth-century writers, is fascinated by the problem of time (Bienek, p. 140). *Billard um halbzehn*, like Thomas Mann's *The Magic Mountain*, is a 'Zeitroman' in two senses: it is a historical novel concerned with the problems of the times, and it is also a novel about the nature of time itself.

In the first place it has a political dimension lacking in the earlier novels and pointing forward to the later ones. Johanna Fähmel attempts to assassinate a Cabinet Minister; Nettlinger and Vacano, prominent ex-Nazis, are now in positions of high office. Schrella, whom they had persecuted in the 1930's is actually arrested on his return to Germany—for his part in the resistance to Hitler. This political dimension is given historical depth in relation not only to the years 1933–45 but to Hindenburg, the epitome of respectability, who made Hitler's government possible, to the inflation of 1923, the 'swindle' perpetuated in 1948, and to Emperor Wilhelm II and his war. Böll's preoccupation here is with the continuity of German history in the worst sense. The 'Lambs', a small anti-Nazi group of the 1930's, continue to be persecuted in the 1950's. However, what is new in this novel is that there is a group at all. Its active resistance is as doomed to failure in 1958 as when Ferdi Progulske tried to assassinate Vacano in 1935. Its members are scattered, some are dead. But the return of Schrella and the adoption of Hugo by Robert are signs that it is being reconstituted. It is not, however, a political grouping—Schrella is 'completely unpolitical'. The political dimension of the novel lies in its rejection of politics.

Continuity and fragmentation are also important in the more general discussion of time. Just as for Proust the 'souvenir involontaire' is the guarantee of the continuity of time, so for Böll it is the individual detail or moment of vision rather than an artificially preserved historical context that is important. Ruth pushes the hair out of her forehead in exactly the way her great-grandmother used to do. Schrella remarks that truth, even a 'tiny corner of truth', can be found only by accumulating thousands of images. In this respect form and content of Böll's novel are congruent, for *Billard um halbzehn* is just such a montage of images.

But it also explores various types of 'timelessness' and

this too is reflected in its structure. Heinrich Fähmel's life has been spent in creating his own 'myth'. There is indeed something of Thomas Mann's young Joseph in Böll's presentation of the young Heinrich Fähmel. From his earliest years he has known exactly what he wants and what he is going to do. Part of his myth consists in eating the same eccentric breakfast in the same café each morning. The relevant characteristic of myth is its timelessness. He remarks : 'I was always so sure of the future that the present appeared to me like the fulfilment of the past.' But myth is an aesthetic category rather than an ethical one. In face of the various catastrophes which he has lived through Heinrich's stance has remained ironic—again echoes of Mann can be heard—not condemning directly, but remaining aloof. He now realises that he has never asked the purpose of his myth. And at the end of the novel he destroys it : he will not attend the rededication of his Abbey, he cancels his breakfast at the Café Kroner. His wife Johanna is a much more resolute person who always spoke her mind. For this reason she has been shut away in a mental hospital since 1942, an image of withdrawal. But the private world of the hospital is a timeless one, since it is a life without responsibilities. And when she orders a taxi by telephone in order to go off to assassinate the Cabinet Minister, she feels 'time streaming back into her face'. The decision to act, a moral one, makes time real once more. Finally, Robert's existence is 'timeless' too. Every morning from 9.30 to 11.00 he plays an abstract game of billiards in a hotel room meditating and reminiscing to Hugo. The world is outside, viewed through a window. His secretary regards him as a machine : all his movements and words seem to be regulated by clockwork. Listening to his stories Hugo finds it difficult sometimes to remember the year they are actually living in. And at the end of the novel he too breaks out of his private, timeless world. Schrella's arrival makes time real again : 'Clocks did not chime in vain, their hands did not move in vain.' Robert adopts Hugo. Friendship and humanity are the acts which give time meaning.

This thematic movement from timelessness to time is directly experienced by the reader. The compression (to about ten hours) and expansion (even into Roman history) found in the time structure of Böll's earlier novels is repeated. But it is mainly in the first half that we feel time to be standing still. The second half brings action, developments, and the pace quickens considerably.[26] This is also a feature of *Haus ohne Hüter* and to a lesser extent of *Und sagte kein einziges Wort*. In this respect too *Billard um halbzehn* culminates the development of Böll's narrative technique.

Böll has frequently been attacked for sentimentality. The central symbols of 'lambs' and 'buffaloes' have come in for particular criticism. This is partly based on a misunderstanding. Böll's lambs are not as meek as the word suggests—some of them are would-be assassins. The leitmotiv phrase, 'Mitleidend bleibt das ewige Herz doch fest' (Suffering in sympathy, the eternal heart will yet stand firm),[27] stresses that pity, feeling for others, must be allied to strength of mind and purpose. The woolly emotionality of Nazi ideologies is one of the objects of Robert Fähmel's scorn.

One way in which Böll tries to balance emotionality is the exact, almost abstract composition of his novel. The network of leitmotivs in this novel is much tighter and more complex than in any of the others. Scarcely a name is mentioned which does not take on significance in the course of the narrative or is not directly related to events. Location is of great structural importance. Everything takes place within sight of the Church of St. Severin—its spire is visible even from Denklingen, the village where Hugo was born and where Johanna's hospital is situated. But the location serves also to establish continuity as a counterpoint to the discontinuity of history. The hotel Prinz Heinrich and the Café Kroner, the Modestgasse, St. Severin have always been there. The river and its banks are especially important. The same sailors' wives who are disembarking when Robert went to the Trischlers in 1935 appear to be present when Joseph and Marianne visit the river bank in 1958. The same ships are doing the same things. The bank is still littered with 'bulrush stems, corks, tins of shoe polish' as when Heinrich first made love to Johanna in 1907. And at the end of the novel the 'Lorries, apprentices, nuns : life in the street' are cancelled out; Gretz has been unable to sell his wild boar carcase—he has hung one outside his shop every day for fifty years—and has to carry it inside again. Things have perhaps changed at the end of this eventful day after all.

4

THE ARTIST NOVELS

As we have seen, the 1960's saw an increasing polarisation between writers and the West German Establishment. The indirect social criticism in the more or less realistic novels of the immediate post-war years gave way to a more direct adopting of political stances. This can be seen especially in the theatre, in the plays for example of Peter Weiss. Turning to politics at once raises the question of the artist's role in society and it is no coincidence that Böll's two major works of the 1960's, *Ansichten eines Clowns* (1963) and *Ende einer Dienstfahrt* (1966) are 'artist novels' in the German tradition of *Wilhelm Meisters Lehrjahre, Der grüne Heinrich* and *Maler Nolten.* Hans Schnier describes himself throughout as an 'artist'. His clowning is his art and the novel describes his relationship to West German society and his conception of his art. The Gruhls of the second novel are less obviously artists, but the act for which they have been brought to trial, the burning of a military jeep, they conceived as a 'happening', the presiding magistrate is convinced of its 'artistic' nature and their punishment is correspondingly light.

The artist's role was a subsidiary theme already of *Haus ohne Hüter.* Martin Bach's father Rai was a poet. When he discovered that the Nazis were using him for propaganda purposes—his poems were good but not obviously anti-Nazi, and were held up to prove that literature could after all flourish under fascism—he devoted himself solely to composing advertisement slogans for his father-in-law's jam factory. In other words, he withdrew into a position resembling that of Böll's eccentrics discussed earlier. Since the war he has become something of a cult figure among Catholics and in cultural circles related to the Restoration, in Böll's terms the second fascism. His protest has not in the end saved him from misuse. Indeed his widow Nella is actively assisting in the cult—until at the end of the novel she breaks away from this kind of society.

As we have seen, *Billard um halbzehn* introduced a political element into Böll's writings. But this many-layered novel is not only a 'Zeitroman', it is also an artist novel, about a family of architects. Heinrich is the constructive architect of a bygone age. His greatest work, St. Anthony's Abbey, built before the First World War, is in the romanesque style and correct in every detail. Robert Fähmel is the contemporary artist—in two ways. As an architect specialising in statics he is, paradoxically, interested mainly in destroying, both during the war when he commanded a demolition squad to open up lines of fire for his mad general, and after it, when he tried to erase all the remnants of the past which had been left standing after the bombing raids and his own activities. One is reminded of the 'Kahlschlag' of German literature immediately after the war, the abjuration of images and ornaments and all those rhetorical devices which Nazi writers had brought into disrepute. The function of the contemporary artist is, it would seem, destructive rather than creative—Böll's demand that art must 'go too far' is related to this.

Both Nazis and Communists have insisted too strongly on the edifying function of literature (*Hierzulande*, p. 55), and Böll's own satires are more effective than the 'positive' features of his work. But Robert is also a portrait of the contemporary artist as billiard-player. His game is 'strict poetry', 'music without melody, painting without an image'. And the abstractness of his billiards game is reflected in the abstractness of the novel itself: the arrival of Nettlinger, of Schrella is like the impact of a billiard ball on the others, setting them in motion, creating new constellations. The similarities between Böll's novel and the *nouveau roman* in France have frequently been indicated,[28] although Böll has poured scorn on the latter (Bienek, p. 148). What has usually been overlooked is that *Billard um halbzehn* is both a 'nouveau roman' and its opposite. For implicit in the novel's ending is an attack on the abstract, purely artistic existence which Robert has been leading.

Unlike his French contemporaries Böll is not strong on theory. The series of four lectures which he delivered at the University of Frankfurt in 1964 as Guest Lecturer in Poetics are rather barren, interesting mainly for providing clues to the writers whom Böll most admires —Adalbert Stifter is mentioned surprisingly frequently and one could draw parallels between Böll's inward-looking anti-society and that depicted by the nineteenth-century writer. They even contain self-contradictory statements, as pointed out by Marcel Reich-Ranicki: at one moment Böll is attacking judgments based on the content of a work of literature, later he protests against purely formalist literature. (Böll replied, justifiably enough, that this contradiction is in the nature of art itself.) (AKR, pp. 506–7; cf. FV, p. 15 and p. 19). One

feature he emphasises on several occasions is the importance of technique, craftsmanship—Heinrich Fähmel too
is not interested in 'art', only in 'craftsmanship'. Critics
who point out technical flaws in his novels are taken
more seriously than those who attack him for the message
they think he is preaching (AKR, p. 509). It must, however, be said that most of his novels do contain flaws
of this kind, as when in *Und sagte kein einziges Wort*
Frau Baluhn later becomes Frau Röder, or when the
time scheme of *Ansichten eines Clowns* breaks down.[29]

Nevertheless, Böll cannot agree with the standpoint
of those critics who know only one responsibility, that
to their art (EHA, p. 427). This is his main criticism of
the *nouveau roman*. Engagement is the whole basis of
his art (Bienek, p. 149) and he refuses to see the political,
the moral and the artistic as alternatives (Arnold, p. 37).
Billard um halbzehn ends with the decision to break out
of the timelessness of the artistic life. Schnier in *Ansichten
eines Clowns* finally leaves the isolation of his flat and
goes off to sing political songs to the people at the
railway station. Böll's own commitment is to 'the
humane' (FV, p. 9); this we have defined in terms of
anti-fascism, anti-bureaucracy, the individualism of the
non-conformist, the man who cannot and will not 'keep
in step' with developments (AKR, pp. 323–4). However,
in a civilisation which is infinitely capable of digesting
all messages so long as they are presented in terms which
can be called 'Art', a civilisation which is both 'museum'
(*Hierzulande,* p. 60) and 'padded cell' (AKR, p. 264),
non-conformist acts are practically impossible, they are
at once classified, pigeon-holed, 'administered'. And the
desperate position of the committed artist is beautifully
illustrated in the ironic endings of both Böll's artist

novels. Schnier puts on his clown's make-up and goes out into the streets. But it is Carnival time, everybody is eccentrically dressed and his appearance is at once assimilated. The Gruhls get off practically scot-free although they have destroyed an army jeep. It was art, a 'happening'. And in any case the court proceedings are kept as quiet as possible, no reporters are present, the wider public hears nothing. Direct action by the artist as artist is shown to be useless. Accordingly *Gruppenbild mit Dame* turns away from the artist again to suggest once more the creation of a counter-society from which established society can be influenced, as it were by guerrilla warfare.

Ansichten eines Clowns had a mixed reception. Indeed, Böll's reputation in the 1960's declined considerably, although his books were invariably best-sellers. This was probably inevitable. Critical opinion is notoriously fickle and after the praise poured on the earlier works a reaction was bound to set in. A curious exception to the general trend was Günter Blöcker, who had been one of Böll's severest critics but gave an enthusiastic review to the Clown.[30] Böll himself views it as one of his weaker works, both because of its sentimentality and because of weaknesses in its construction (Arnold, p. 38). In sentimentality it indeed approaches that of *Der Zug war pünktlich* : tears, hot and cold, are shed copiously, occasionally to music, this time that of Chopin played over the telephone.

Like *Und sagte kein einziges Wort* it is a first person narrative about a broken marriage—for Schnier regards himself as Marie's legitimate husband, although they were never officially married—and the Catholic Establishment plays an even greater role as villain. Again it is not an autobiography in the accepted sense—Schnier is not looking back at the past in the manner of one writing his memoirs—but an interior monologue. The narrative time covers about three hours, if one disregards the inconsistencies, and past events are narrated by means of flash-backs as Schnier meditates on how he has reached the state he is in. In this reduction of narrative time, *Ansichten eines Clowns* goes further than any of Böll's novels and most closely fulfils his ambition of telling a novel 'in one minute' in order to show the inextricable relationship of past and present (Bienek, p. 145).

As in the earlier novel mirrors play an important part, not only to give a visual impression of the narrator but in order to underline his isolation. More important in the latter respect, however, is location, once more of structural significance. As with time we find in this novel the most radical reduction of location. Practically the whole novel is set in Schnier's flat in Bonn. The importance of a brief encounter with a neighbour on the landing outside is highlighted by this fact alone. He is visited by his father but there is no communication between them—indeed for much of the time Schnier is dreaming and not listening to what his father is saying. Otherwise his only contact with the outside world is by the telephone. About one-fifth of the novel is taken up with telephone conversations, whose beginning or end frequently forms the basis of the chapter divisions. The characteristic development found at the close of all Böll's novels is here expressed spatially in Schnier's moving outwards from his flat to participate in the world outside. Expansion in space, as in time, is conveyed through flashbacks. But as Schnier's life has been spent predominantly in hotel rooms and various types of theatre, the overwhelming impression remains one of interiors, suggesting the self and the artist's ivory tower, the position which he attempts to overcome at the end.

The adult protagonists of Böll's previous novels were all about the age of their author. Schnier was born much later, about 1934. He was only ten at the end of the war. Clearly an elderly clown suffering from a broken heart would be less plausible and even more sentimental. Nevertheless, it is difficult to dissociate in one's mind the 'I' of the narrative from Böll the author—although on his own testimony for autobiographical references he would prefer the third person.[31] At times one feels Böll wrote the novel because he, as much as Schnier, 'was furious with Catholicism and Catholics'. There is too little sense of distance. Much of his portrait of the artist as a young man applies very clearly to himself. Schnier's scorn of 'artistic people' takes up a theme of Böll's other works and essays. His refusal to accept the advice of the professional critic Genneholm reflects Böll's own attitude; Schnier is influenced only on the private level, for example, by the General's wife, who makes him give up his most successful act. The clown's analysis of his own strengths and weaknesses seems relevant to Böll himself and suggests that Böll was stock-taking at this point. 'All my attempts at the lyrical had failed.' Not until 1972 did Böll publish poems; the poetic prose of *Der Zug war pünktlich* fails to come off; he is more successful in this mode in the poetic evocation of East European landscapes in *Wo warst du, Adam?* 'I had never yet succeeded in presenting the humane without producing frightful *kitsch*.' With some reservations this is true of Böll's works: his villains, tending towards the caricature, are often more credible than positive figures like Käte Bogner—in fact, since Käte the positive figures have usually been dead (Leen, Edith) and thus softened in outline by distance and perspective. 'I am best at presenting everyday absurdities.' Satire like *Nicht nur zur Weihnachtszeit, Doktor Murkes gesammeltes Schweigen* and *Der Wegwerfer* do precisely that and must be ranked among Böll's most unreservedly successful works.

More interesting still is Schnier's statement to his brother Leo towards the end of the novel: 'I'm a clown . . . and I collect moments.' Each of his turns represents a significant moment in ordinary life, an 'epiphany', to use the Joycean term. Elsewhere he claims that it is the detail which brings home to one the whole horror of events. He remembers in particular the moment when Henriette, wearing her blue hat, went off in the tram to fight the 'Jewish Yankees'. Böll's works are full of such 'epiphanies', brief moments of vision which suddenly make life meaningful, from the 'tenth of a second' in which Andreas's eyes met those of a French girl near Amiens (*Der Zug war pünktlich*) through the unexpected encounter of Fred Bogner with his wife in the street which prompts him to return home, to the glance exchanged between Albert and Heinrich's mother at the end of *Haus ohne Hüter* and the 'love at first sight' theme of *Das Brot der frühen Jahre*. The many leitmotivs of *Billard um halbzehn* could also be mentioned. In *Ansichten eines Clowns* itself what is perhaps the one ray of light in an otherwise deeply pessimistic novel is the chance meeting of Schnier and his neighbour on the landing. The short stories are frequently based on such an encounter. Böll's favourite literary form is the short story and one of the most satisfying definitions of the genre is as an 'epiphany', a momentary encounter with life.

According to Böll the submerged form of *Ansichten eines Clowns* is the story of Theseus and Ariadne. Schnier is Theseus, the artist in the labyrinth of a modern bureaucratic state, more specifically the Catholic Establishment; Marie is Ariadne, she has cut the thread and left him to find his way out.[32] This interpretation seems rather to take us away from the story. It is much more useful to view Marie Derkum as a personification of post-war West Germany and the novel as an allegory of the artist's 'affair' with his country. After living for some time in uneasy concubinage with the artist, Germany has, probably finally, gone over to the Catholic Establishment. The novel is more directly political than any of Böll's other novels. Names are mentioned, Strauss, Erhard, Adenauer (against the mysterious 'Herr M.' of *Billard um halbzehn*). The town is Bonn, capital of the Federal Republic, rather than the disguised Cologne of the earlier works. Marie's father is a Communist without a party, a member of the 'homeless Left' whose post-war hopes have been dashed by the development of both political parties. Her honeymoon with Züpfner is spent in Rome and the Rome-Bonn axis ominously echoes an earlier Rome-Berlin axis. Marie is a rather shadowy figure whom we never meet directly. Her respect for 'culture' and her apparent inability to bear children are qualities which can easily be interpreted allegorically. The level of pure realism is pierced on several occasions —Schnier can detect smells over the telephone—and the flatness of so many of the characters is a common feature of allegory.

Ende einer Dienstfahrt was given a luke-warm reception by the critics, who saw it as a slight work suggesting that Böll was sinking into provincialism. The latter accusation provokes Böll to wrath, not because he denies his provincialism, but because he cannot see it as a fault: the greatest novelists have been firmly anchored in a specific geographical locality (FV, p. 16). It is certainly the most humorous and relaxed of all Böll's longer works. Böll feels it has been underestimated; the 'demand for action' in the 'happening' has been overlooked (Arnold, p. 34).

One outstanding feature must be noted at the outset, since it is clear from the first sentence of the story: 'At the magistrate's court in Birglar in the early autumn of last year a case was heard of whose outcome the public heard very little.' The narrative point of view is not that of one of the characters—it is a third-person narrative—but that of an external, anonymous narrator, 'omniscient' in a way, since he knows what nobody else can know. It is a very impersonal point of view: no judgments are passed or moral statements made as at the beginning of *Der Zug war pünktlich*. Traces of this much more traditional narrative technique are to be found in some of the earlier novels, notably *Wo warst du, Adam?*, but never to this extent and never at the beginning. The treatment of time is similarly more traditional than in the previous works. There is a straightforward plot with a beginning and an ending corresponding to those of the court proceedings. Instead of the 'open' beginning of all Böll's longer stories up to now, in which we are plunged into the middle of events related with reference to an unexplained 'he', 'she' or 'I', we find precise information

on what we are about to hear; where it happened, when
it happened and an odd feature of what happened.

This radical break with past habits is disconcerting.
There is of course no law which compels a writer to
adopt one narrative technique rather than another. But
the consistency of the previous novels in their abjuration
of an archimedean point of view from which the world
can be explained, reformed, moved, leads one to ask how
Böll has suddenly discovered one. H. J. Bernhard rightly
points out that the narrator here has the function of
revealing the truth which the ruling powers are so
anxious to hide.[33] Clearly the story demands such a
narrator. But one can perhaps go further and say that
the anonymity of this narrator is parallel to the faceless-
ness of Grellber, the mysterious 'President' in whose
hands the strings manipulating the puppets are held.
Bureaucracy has become total, fascist in fact, and desperate measures, guerrilla warfare is demanded.

Bureaucracy takes three main forms in this novel: as
the legal system, as the army and as the taxation system.
The 'Staatsanwalt' in this case is not merely the pros-
ecuting counsel but, literally, the 'apologist of the
State'. No citizen has anything to fear from the State,
he declares, as long as he observes its laws. He even
defends the Nazi State in these terms. Stollfuss, the
presiding magistrate, admits in his closing speech the
complete helplessness of human justice in this case, that
is justice administered by the law. Stollfuss is humane,
on the verge of retirement, quite different from the
unrepentant Nazi Kugl-Egger. However, he too is part
of a system ruled by the faceless Grellber.—The criti-
cisms levelled by Böll at the army as institution in his
earliest works are repeated here especially the 'boredom'

65

and 'meaninglessness' of army life. However, the army is especially equated with bureaucracy, in its organisation and in its activities. No war is being fought and like other branches of the administration the army tends to spend much of its time justifying its own existence. The 'official journey' of the novel's title refers to the practice of sending army vehicles on long journeys across the countryside with the sole purpose of registering sufficient mileage in time for the regular inspection.— The taxation system may well have been the initial impulse for Böll's novel. In an article for *Die Zeit* in 1963 Böll attacked the government's proposals for taxing writers: requiring no material other than paper and pencil, having no overhead expenses, such as wages for employees, unable to invest in weighty capital equipment, all of which they could set off against tax, they were yet going to be taxed on the same basis as industrial firms, de facto at a higher rate (AKR, pp. 460–3). Gruhl senior is the artist equivalent in this respect. The tax system has ruined him, the small, independent craftsman, and Grähn, the taxation specialist, can only shake his head in astonishment that he has survived at all.

The underlying pattern of the novel is another traditional feature. The courtroom novel is a subdivision of detective fiction. For Böll's purposes it is brilliantly apt. In his other novels the subsidiary characters are introduced through the medium of a main character's mind. Fred and Käte Bogner evoke Frau Franke and the Bishop; Albert, Nella and Frau Brielach their dead spouses; Schnier literally calls up his various acquaintances—by telephone. The courtroom novel does not have to resort to such means: the witnesses are called to the witness box by the presiding magistrate, they appear in the flesh, are interrogated and dismissed. And *Ende einer Dienstfahrt* is remarkable for the collection of living individuals it presents. There is necessarily more direct speech and Böll is able to make great play with the speech registers of the various professions represented. Böll's characters have always been almost as much preoccupied with the past as with the present. The interrogation of witnesses is precisely concerned with unveiling the past—and Böll even succeeds in bringing the war into this novel too. The time structure is again one of compression—to the single day of the proceedings—and expansion. So too with location—from the courtroom to the various scenes of the Gruhls' activities.

There is another important location, however, besides the courtroom, namely the several inns and restaurants in which the central section takes place during the lunch interval. If the courtroom represents the bureaucratic sphere, these point to a much more optimistic feature of the novel. The Gruhls, unlike Schnier, unlike even the Fähmels, are not alone. They belong to a community, provincial, even rural. Birglar and its environs lacks the dubious features noted in *Haus ohne Hüter*'s Bietenhahn and is presented in much greater depth. Its name is significant. Birglar is the place where something is 'hidden' (bergen = hide). It was chosen by the administration as the scene of the court proceedings in order to hush up the whole affair. But it is also the place where the last vestiges of humane, anti-bureaucratic civilisation are concealed. Eating was for Schrella a communal activity. And so it is for the local patrons whether of the Café Frohn or of the Duhr-Terrassen. Even in prison

67

the Gruhls are not forgotten, but eat of the best the Duhr-Terrassen can provide. And the tables are turned on the administration, for it is not the Gruhls who are the outsiders here, as Böll's earlier protagonists were, but Bergnolte, Grellber's representative, and Heimüller, the least agreeable member of the Bundeswehr, who are very clearly shown that they do not belong. To return to the narrative point of view: there *is* a standpoint which is not purely individualist, that of the small local community based on mutual respect and friendship.

5

GRUPPENBILD MIT DAME

Böll's output has slackened in the past decade. Whereas the fifties saw the publication of four novels and numerous collections of short and longer stories, the sixties produced only two novels, one of which, *Ende einer Dienstfahrt*, Böll describes as an 'Erzählung', and only a few shorter works. Apart from *Ende einer Dienstfahrt*, *Gruppenbild mit Dame* (1971) was Böll's first novel since *Ansichten eines Clowns* appeared eight years earlier. However, this is not a question of a reduction in creative ideas. The most recent novel is his longest and his richest, both in the vast gallery of characters and in the wealth of incident and historical depth which it presents. Critical opinion was, as usual, mixed. Karl Korn pronounced it 'probably Böll's most significant book';[34] Marcel Reich-Ranicki dismissed it as 'a weak book'.[35] Most critics were rather puzzled by its mixture of the old Böll and some new elements. This did not prevent it from rapidly becoming Böll's most successful novel, selling 150,000 copies in six months and, helped by the award of the Nobel prize, continuing to be prominent in the best-seller lists a year and a half after its appearance.

Gruppenbild mit Dame includes all the old themes of Böll's works. Once more we are taken into the now no longer quite so immediate past, the 1930's, the war, the post-war years up the present-day concrete jungles of a German city. Anti-militarism, anti-clericalism are important. The anti-cultural theme is repeated, but in modified form, for literary allusions are a dominant feature of the leitmotiv patterns and symbolism of the novel. The well-known characters reappear: the opportunists rather than the downright criminal among the antagonists, the mixture of the angelic and the sensual in the protagonists. The non-conformists, the social outsiders are once more threatened by contemporary society, whether it be the Nazis before 1945 or the present-day property owners who wish to 'develop' a valuable plot of ground in the city which has become the refuge of war-widows and foreign workers. Motifs of earlier works are repeated: the graveyards of *Und sagte kein einziges Wort* and *Es wird etwas geschehen*, the stealing of gold fillings from the teeth of corpses from one of Böll's early war stories.

On the first reading one is bewildered by the multiplicity of characters—indeed, Helmut Heissenbüttel, in a subtle and positive review confuses Margret Schlömer and Marja van Doorn,[36] and Hans Schwab-Felisch admitted that he could only cope by drawing up a list of the characters as they appeared.[37] Towards the end the novel threatens to disintegrate, when the narrator falls in love with a nun and leads her back into the world. Böll's earlier novels often end on an artificial, melodramatic note. *Gruppenbild mit Dame* makes no such concession to the 'need for an ending'; it peters out; one feels that it could go on for ever. Böll's inventive powers never fail him. Each time our attention begins to slacken, a new grotesque or satirical episode—always Böll's strength—is introduced: the fictitious Russian workers with literary names in Hubert Gruyten's vast swindle; the detailed description of wreath-making; Pelzer's profiteering on funerals by using the same coffins, wreaths, even inscriptions again and again; the Hoysers' ultra-modern office block whose inmates are slaves to the over-sensitive air-conditioning system; the traffic jam caused by refuse lorries to save Leni from eviction; the death of Margret, the prostitute—from blushing.

Despite the apparent chaos, important structural principles can be detected. These are basically similar to the ones employed by Böll in his earlier novels : the past is revealed through a relatively brief passage of time in the present, and this is done by a montage of points of view. But there are significant differences, all of which can be traced to the figure of the Biographer, which Böll introduces for the first time.

Through his presence the time structure receives an additional dimension. For the novel is not only about the group of people referred to in the title, it is also about the writing of a novel about this group of people. And on both levels we see the characteristic two-part form of Böll's novels. They begin with a lengthy exposition, the description of a situation in depth, interpreted in relation to the past; this is followed by a relatively brief 'action', in which the situation is developed and a new constellation of circumstances created. In *Gruppenbild mit Dame* the term 'first section', which the Biographer uses on two occasions, implies this structure. Although he never mentions a second section, this must begin in the middle of Chapter 9. It is marked in Leni's case by the sudden imminence of her eviction and Schirtenstein's creation of the 'Help-

Leni-Committee', in the Biographer's case by his increasingly direct involvement with the people he is
describing, his love affair with Klementina and his first
direct encounter with Leni.

Gruppenbild mit Dame is a much more rambling
novel than anything Böll had written previously. It is
odd that a break between two sections should occur in
the middle of a chapter; in fact it is not always easy to
understand the basis for the chapter divisions as they
stand. The chapters of Böll's earlier novels usually begin
with a change of perspective. *Ansichten eines Clowns*,
like *Gruppenbild mit Dame* related by a single narrator,
is much more arbitrary in its chapter divisions, but is
held together by the extreme condensation of its narrative time. The narrative time of the latest novel is
left vague. We cannot determine how long the Biographer spends on his researches. Suffice it to note that,
in contrast to the conventional biographical novel, the
events told by the Biographer are still happening. He is
not giving a summary of his findings but rather an
account of them as they take place. As with *Ansichten
eines Clowns* and *Und sagte kein einziges Wort* there is
no absolute past.

In this novel the past is evoked not by flash-backs or
interior monologues but by eye-witness accounts of the
people interviewed by the Biographer in the course of
his researches. Thus the montage of points of view is
repeated even here. *Ende einer Dienstfahrt* anticipates
the technique. But whereas there the montage was linked
by an anonymous narrator, the only feature of whose
personality was that he was telling the story at all, against
the express wishes of the authorities, in *Gruppenbild mit
Dame* the narrator, still anonymous, is endowed with

recognisable characteristics, a past history and a set of definable values, and he actually interferes in the story he is telling, helping to make the lives of Margret and Bogakov more bearable, contributing to the aid-fund for Leni, inducing one of the witnesses, Klementina, to leave her nunnery. We hear of his running battle with the tax authorities over his expense account. His anti-Nazi, anti-militarist, anti-nationalist stance is obvious on several occasions. He is not averse to commenting on events and in some ways resembles a traditional narrator.

Nevertheless, he is at pains to emphasise his 'objectivity' throughout. He is 'incapable of inventing or lying', 'dependent on facts'. *Gruppenbild mit Dame* is a kind of documentary novel with a place in a growing German tradition particularly popular in the contemporary distrust of 'fiction'. Hans Magnus Enzensberger's *Der kurze Sommer der Anarchie* (1972) is a collection of documents and some commentaries on the life of an anarchist leader in the Spanish Civil War. In its treatment of 'facts' Böll's novel is, however, closer to the playfulness of Alfred Döblin's *Berlin Alexanderplatz*. The Biographer reproduces a number of 'documents', some fictitious, like the literary effusions of Alois Pfeiffer or the expert's report on the character of Lev, others genuine, relating to Nazi atrocities or military regulations. This claim to historical truth has two sides. When the narrator himself admits that it is, to say the least, improbable that a Russian prisoner-of-war should enjoy the protection of an anonymous German diplomat and should meet Leni under the conditions and with the results described in the novel, our objections are disarmed. But of course this is merely one of a series of ironic refractions in the novel. For *Gruppenbild mit Dame* is really a parody of the genre it purports to belong to. The solemn experimental testing of trivialities like the duration of the 'deathly silence' which followed Leni's first offer of coffee to Boris is calculated to cast doubt on all claims to scientific objectivity, for example that of the expert's report on Lev's character. Conversely, the miracle of the roses which spring from Rahel's ashes takes on more plausibility by virtue of its being hotly denied by the Church.

Much of the irony is conveyed through register. It takes several forms, from the parody of various kinds of jargon, theological, existentialist, sociological, military, through the anti-ideological—Lotte's husband does not 'fall' in action, he is 'dropped'—to the Biographer's own deliberately unliterary, even anti-literary style. A foretaste of the latter was given in *Entfernung von der Truppe* (1964), which also contains a number of themes developed in *Gruppenbild mit Dame*, the excremental, the nuns, includes a montage of documents and plays with the more fashionable terms of literary criticism like 'change of narrative level' and Lessing's concept of the 'time art'. In the novel the abbreviation 'Verf.', which the Biographer uses throughout to refer to himself, is a similar parody of literary scholarship. The unattractive colloquialisms and banalities of his own style contrast radically with the almost liturgical rhythms of parts of *Billard um halbzehn* and can only be understood in the light of the anti-aesthetic stance in this novel. At one point he solemnly consults his encyclopaedia for definitions of terms like 'tears', 'laughter', 'suffering', 'happiness'. Thereafter these terms almost always appear in abbreviated form—as in the encyclopaedia. On the one hand this is parody, implying an attack on useless definitions of basic human emotions. On the other, it is a kind of 'alienation effect', which allows him to include what otherwise would be unbearably sentimental—the danger has been present, as we have seen, in all Böll's works. Böll's monism has never been clearer than in this novel. The physical and the emotional are one, hence the overwhelming importance of tears, excrementa, orgasms and blushing.

Because of the unifying presence of the Biographer, leitmotiv patterns are less important than in the earlier novels. But Böll has created a complex system of symbols and literary allusions. An exhaustive interpretation of these would demand a book in itself. The more salient ones can be mentioned. The graveyard vaults in which the last weeks of the war are spent evoke the catacombs of the early Christians. The last months of Rahel, the Jewish nun, are spent in similar seclusion, hidden from the Nazis, and in daily expectation of the arrival of the Lord. The withdrawal of Böll's protagonists is related to the situation of the early Christians in a hostile world. Leni's son, Lev, has come in conflict with the State and Grundtsch offers to hide him in the vaults where he was born: the contemporary German administration is by analogy fascist.

Two of Leni's lodgers are called Hans and Grete. The Hänsel and Gretel theme implies that Leni is to be seen as the witch. Witches are mentioned by the industrial psychologist in his testimony on the character of Leni's son Lev: he quotes a modern study of witchcraft which tries to explain the 'beauty' and 'sexual attractiveness' of witches and their 'understanding of the internal secretory processes'. Leni is sexually attractive and internal secretory processes play an important part in her life. Like the historical witches she is 'ahead of her time' in this. She is rejected by the orthodox Establishment and submitted to a kind of 'Inquisition'. But unlike the witch of the folk-tale, reputed by the no doubt jealous citizens to devour children, Leni gives refuge to those who, like herself, are social rejects.

Leni's favourite reading includes a curious mixture of poems by Hölderlin, Trakl and Brecht. Hölderlin's poem 'In my boyhood days' has an obvious bearing on Leni's affair with Boris in the wreath-making business: 'And learned to love / Amid the flowers.'[38] Trakl's 'lyrics of decay' reflect the general atmosphere of decadence and the world coming to an end; Brecht is related to the strong undercurrent of Communism in the novel. Kleist's *Die Marquise von O.* is frequently mentioned, no doubt because a Russian officer is the central male figure. Some of the scenes during the bombing raids remind one much more forcibly of the same author's *Das Erdbeben in Chili*. Leni's position in a hostile world, her trust in the Madonna and her extreme sensuality, is implied in the words quoted from Kafka's *Ein Landarzt* (A Country Doctor): 'with earthly carriage, unearthly horses'. Most interesting of all is the one poem quoted in full, sung by Leni alone in her flat as the committee set up to help her is about to begin its work next door. It can be identified as a free-verse German translation of the poem *A Coat* by Yeats. The poem represents Yeats's repudiation of the Celtic Twilight's ornamental Romantic mythologies and his turning to a more austere style of poetry.[39] Germany too has had its share of mythologies—disastrously. Böll's abjuration of the more obviously artistic effects in this novel is reflected in the poem. But it also relates to

Leni, whose career has been inextricably bound up with her country. 'The most German girl of the school', she married a Nazi, but was for a brief time after the war a member of the Communist Party. Now she rejects all commitment to any political party : 'For there's more enterprise / In walking naked.'

Leni is devoid of ideology, but she is not devoid of helpers. *Gruppenbild mit Dame* continues the optimistic strain of *Ende einer Dienstfahrt*. The final scenes sketch a bizarre commune of some fourteen people, who include a music critic, the proprietor of a flower shop, a civil servant, a rich capitalist, Turkish and Portuguese foreign workers, a Russian ex-prisoner-of-war and a retired graveyard attendant, all devoted to the defence of Leni. The scene, we are told, is reminiscent of that of the conspiracy in St. Petersburg in October 1917. The Russian element is strong throughout the novel. Böll's alternative society has nothing to do with present-day Communism in its historical form. But it has every-thing to do with the spirit which inspired the original revolution. And in this novel, at least temporarily, it triumphs over the combined forces of bureaucracy and profiteering capitalism.

Böll's alternative society is expanding. But to what extent does it pose a threat to the established order? Little acts of sabotage such as the scene with the refuse lorries will have no more permanent effect than the Gruhls' demonstration—it too is referred to as a 'hap-pening' in the newspaper report. The Hoysers have been thwarted—for the moment. More conclusive is the Biographer's affair with Klementina, which at a first reading seems so extraneous. If *Gruppenbild mit Dame* is really the 'novel of a novel' then it must also be a kind of artist novel, like its two predecessors. There are various artist figures in it. Leni's brother Heinrich and her cousin Erhard, both executed by firing squad during the war for sabotage, were poets, as was Alois Pfeiffer, her Nazi husband. Leni herself belongs to this category. Her wreath-making, we are told, was highly artistic. More recently she has been drawing a large-scale trans-verse-section of one of the layers of the retina of Rahel's left eye. Bizarre? Only partly, if one remembers how important for Böll the writer's eye for detail is (EHA, p. 339). But the most important artist-figure is the Biographer himself, and his departure from neutrality and strict objectivity in the course of the novel is similar to and of more permanent significance than, for example, Schnier's taking up his position on the steps of Bonn station.

Klementina is persuaded to leave her nunnery. We remember that entering a monastery was one solution suggested in *Nicht nur zur Weihnachtszeit*. In this motif we can see perhaps most clearly how Böll has progressed since his beginnings. Ilona of *Wo warst du, Adam?* had intended to become a nun, but her yearn-ings for a husband and children induced her to return to the world—where she is killed. Her attitude—prayer to console God—remains that of the nunnery, pure inwardness. In *Und sagte kein einziges Wort* the monks in the procession are particularly photogenic, there is an implication of superficiality and hypocrisy. But their liturgical chants are one of the few things that correspond to the mongol child's purer reality—again withdrawal is viewed positively. In *Haus ohne Hüter* the church of the nuns is one of Albert's favourite haunts. How-ever, Bolda has been a nun, only to return to the world again; and films with nuns in them are suitable for adults only, Martin finds, they belong, in terms of the novel, to the Establishment. By *Billard um halbzehn* Böll's attitude has changed considerably. The monks of St. Anthony's Abbey sang Nazi songs and took part in the Nazi celebrations of the summer solstice. Even after the war they are more ready to be reconciled to the Nazis than to the Communist East. In *Ansichten eines Clowns* the Catholic college where Hans Schnier's brother is training for the priesthood is again a negative symbol. Klementina's return into the world is therefore an important statement of Böll's position. Withdrawal is no longer adequate; the offensive must begin.

6

CONCLUSION

Böll is primarily a writer of narrative fiction. He has tried his hand at other genres. The immediate post-war years saw the blossoming of the radio play in Germany. Like the short story it was an economical and technically modern means of expression. Moreover, the broadcasting stations were in these years most important patrons of the arts, affording financial security to many writers, including Böll, until they had established themselves. In the 1950's Böll wrote a handful of plays for this medium and he has continued to contribute, most recently in *Hausfriedensbruch* and *Aussatz*. The themes are similar to those of the narrative works, the presentation is fairly conventional. *Aussatz* he later turned into a stage play, but without much success. An earlier play, *Ein Schluck Erde* (A Mouthful of Earth) (1961) was a catastrophic failure and had to be dropped after three performances. Böll's distrust of the worn-out clichés of contemporary language had led him to invent a primitive jargon which merely provoked laughter. Most recently a slim volume of poems appeared (1972). But again these are interesting more in relation to Böll's other works than for their intrinsic value.

Let us therefore conclude with a brief assessment of Böll's position as a novelist in relation to his contemporaries and to the German narrative tradition. His early reputation was made in relation to the 'Gruppe 47', whose prize he received in 1951. Founded by Hans Werner Richter in 1947, this extremely loose association of writers arose out of the left-wing circle around Richter and Alfred Andersch which published a journal *Der Ruf* (1946–7) dedicated to the propagation of 'socialist humanism', non-Marxist, critical both of the 'collective guilt' thesis of the Americans and the dogmatic Communism of the Russians, pleading for European unity and the socialisation of the means of production. Many of these themes recur in Böll's works. A writer to whom he was frequently compared in the early 1950's was Wolfgang Borchert, whose early death had helped to make him into something of a cult figure of the time. Borchert's stories strike us today as unbearably sentimental, much more so even than Böll's; but Borchert's stylised anti-stylisation effect is found also in the early Böll, the love, for example, of repetitions of words or phrases. The fragmentation of Böll's novels, the montage effect of a variety of points of view, is a common feature of the post-war German novel, employed for example by Wolfgang Koeppen (*Tauben im Gras*, 1951) and Alfred Andersch (*Sansibar oder Der letzte Grund*, 1957). *Billard um halbzehn*'s relation to the *nouveau roman* has already been mentioned; the interior monologues were said at the time to derive from the now largely forgotten Wolfgang Koeppen. It appeared in 1959, the year which saw the emergence of two important new novelists, Günter Grass with *Die Blechtrommel* (The Tin Drum) and Uwe Johnson with *Mutmassungen über Jakob*. Johnson is much too humourless to be properly compared with Böll; nevertheless, *Gruppenbild mit Dame* might have been entitled 'Mutmassungen über Leni'—conjectures about Leni; in both novels the central character is perceived mainly at second hand. Grass is the most serious rival. Nothing Böll has written has quite the epic vitality of *Die Blechtrommel* or parts of *Hundejahre* (Dog Years). *Gruppenbild mit Dame* comes closest to it, perhaps. Indeed there seem to be allusions to or influences of Grass's novels in the theme of the excremental of the nuns in Böll's novel. Traces of the contemporary trend to the documentary novel in *Gruppenbild mit Dame* have already been noted.

One of the themes of Böll's essays is the irreparable destruction which Nazi rule has wrought on German traditions. School life is invariably presented negatively in Böll's works; for schools are concerned with preserving traditions. The Schillerian idealism of the distych to the heroes of Thermopylae :

> Wanderer, kommst du nach Sparta, verkündige dorten, du habest
>
> Uns hier liegen gesehn, wie das Gesetz es befahl
>
> (Traveller, if you come to Sparta, report there that you saw us lying here, as the law commanded)

has literally been snapped off, as the title of Böll's first collection of short stories indicates. Writers in the early post-war years felt themselves to be groping in the dark, unable to connect with anything that had previously been written. Not even the German language was above suspicion, writes Wolfdietrich Schnurre,[40] and Böll's preoccupation with language has been illustrated again and again.

Accordingly, Böll's novels do not obviously belong to the main tradition of the German novel, a fact which may well account for the suspicion with which they are

regarded in certain academic and critical quarters.
Thematically, elements of the 'artist novels' of the nineteenth century may be recognised. But in general com-
parison with the 'Entwicklungsroman' tradition of the
eighteenth and nineteenth centuries, the novel which
traces the development of a representative individual in
his relation to the outside world, is unfruitful. Nor is
there any point of contact between Böll's novels and
the ponderous philosophical novels of Thomas Mann,
Hermann Broch or Robert Musil in the first half of the
present century.

Nevertheless, they do relate to an equally long, if
submerged tradition, one which has been admirably
analysed by Herman Meyer in his book on the eccentrics
of German literature.[41] Tracing them back to the
'Fools' of medieval literature, Meyer has shown how in
the course of the nineteenth century the eccentric individual took on a new significance. For Stifter and
Keller true originality, that is, individuality, personality,
was still possible only in submission to certain objective
social demands. But by the second part of the century,
in the later works of Wilhelm Raabe, these social demands, indeed society itself, had become a completely
negative concept and true humanity was to be found
only against society, in the private sphere of an eccentric
individual. There are many interesting parallels between
Raabe's works and those of Böll : the intertwining of past
and present, the regrets at missed opportunities after a
war—in Raabe's case the 1870–1 war against the
French. And Böll's protest against the computerised
world falls into the same pattern as Raabe's attack on
the materialist, superficial and standardised society of
his day. Society is not only negative, it is irredeemable.

The revolt of the men with the eccentric professions in the stories of the 1950's is a purely private one. Even later action remains ineffective. Johanna Fähmel's attempt to assassinate a Minister fails—of course. The Gruhls' demonstration against the Bundeswehr is art, therefore acceptable; in any case it is all hushed up by the authorities. The best that Böll can offer is the creation of an alternative society on the personal, individual level. In this there is a development in his works. His early characters are isolated and practically friendless. The married couple may form a nucleus of resistance but it is a very precarious one in *Und sagte kein einziges Wort* and only hinted at at the close of *Haus ohne Hüter.* Adoption of an orphan in *Billard um halbzehn* is a similarly private gesture. Hans Schnier of *Ansichten eines Clowns* is perhaps the loneliest of all Böll's characters, with only the telephone to connect him to the outside world. The inner monologues which are the outstanding feature of Böll's narrative technique up to this novel point to this isolation of the characters. *Ende einer Dienstfahrt* marks a widening of Böll's concept of a community in opposition to society. Camus's alternatives, 'solitaire' or 'solidaire', have been resolved in favour of the latter.[42] *Gruppenbild mit Dame* continues and develops this concept. The revolutionary commune, the community presented at the end of this novel is no longer merely a provincial German one, but an international one, uniting the underdogs of all nations, whether they be Russian prisoners-of-war or Turkish or Portuguese foreign workers.

NOTES

NOTES

1 *Die Welt*, 20.10.1972.
2 *Der Spiegel* 15 (1961), No. 50, pp. 71–2.
3 See Frank Grützbach (ed.): *Freies Geleit für Ulrike Meinhof. Ein Artikel und seine Folgen,* Cologne: Kiepenheuer & Witsch 1972.
4 See Hans Werner Richter (ed.): *Die Mauer oder Der 13. August,* Reinbek: Rowohlt 1961, especially pp. 123 ff.
5 The following abbreviations are used in the text: AKR = *Aufsätze, Kritiken, Reden*; EHA = *Erzählungen, Hörspiele, Aufsätze*; Arnold = *Im Gespräch: Heinrich Böll mit Heinz Ludwig Arnold,* Munich: Boorberg 1971 (Edition Text + Kritik); Bienek = Horst Bienek: *Werkstattgespräche mit Schriftstellern,* Munich: Hanser 1962; FV = *Frankfurter Vorlesungen*; *Hierzulande* = *Hierzulande. Aufsätze zur Zeit.*
6 *Text + Kritik,* No. 33, p. 11.
7 See Günter Wirth: *Heinrich Böll. Essayistische Studie über religiöse und gesellschaftliche Motive im Prosawerk des Dichters,* Cologne: Pahl-Rugenstein 1969, Chapter 1.
8 'Wo ist dein Bruder?', in *Geist und Tat,* 11 (1956), pp. 165–71.
9 Böll-Warnach: 'Die unverlierbare Geschichte. Ein Gespräch', in: *Labyrinth,* 2 (1961), No. 3/4, p. 58.

10 See *Der Spiegel*, 26 (1972), No. 43, pp. 65–6.

11 AKR, pp. 483–7. Benn's words are in 'Lebensweg eines Intellektualisten' (1934).

12 *Der Schriftsteller Heinrich Böll. Ein biographisch-bibliographischer Abriss*, ed. Werner Lengning (3rd edn., Munich: DTV 1972) wrongly dates *Auch Kinder sind Zivilisten, Mein teures Bein, Wir Besenbinder* and *An der Brücke* as first appearing in 1950. They all appeared in the periodical *Der Ruf*, the first three in 1948, the last in 1949.

13 The critical terminology used is that of Elizabeth Boa and J. H. Reid: *Critical Strategies. German Fiction in the Twentieth Century*, London: Arnold 1972.

14 *Strahlungen*, Tübingen: Heliopolis 1949, p. 224.

15 *In Stahlgewittern. Ein Kriegstagebuch*, 21st edn., Berlin: Mittler 1941, p. 10, p. 95.

16 Hans Joachim Bernhard must be contradicted when he writes of Andreas overcoming his isolation in conversations with his two travelling companions (*Die Romane Heinrich Bölls. Gesellschaftskritik und Gemeinschaftsutopie*, Berlin: Rütten & Loening 1970, p. 21).

17 Cf. René Wellek: 'The Concept of Realism in Literary Scholarship', in *Concepts of Criticism*, New Haven: Yale U.P., 1963.

18 Hans Joachim Bernhard over-emphasises the role of the narrator in this novel (op. cit., pp. 47 f.). His conception of the narrator is too undifferentiated.

19 W. A. Coupe: 'Heinrich Böll's *Und sagte kein einziges Wort*—An analysis' in *German Life and Letters*, 17 (1963/64), p. 243.

20 See Rolf Dahrendorf: *Gesellschaft und Demokratie in Deutschland*, Munich: Piper 1965, pp. 341–59.

21 Theodore Ziolkowski does not mention this novel in his article 'The Odysseus Theme in recent German Fiction' (*Comparative Literature,* 14 (1962), pp. 225-41). But he does draw attention to Böll's words on Odysseus in 'Bekenntnis zur Trümmerliteratur' (EHA, p. 343).

22 *Deutsche Dichtung der Gegenwart,* Frankfurt a.M. : Athenäum 1953, p. 442.

23 Loc. cit., p. 248.

24 *Revue des deux Mondes,* 1.11.1960, p. 164.

25 *The Times,* 1.6.1961.

26 Cf. Therese Poser: 'Heinrich Böll—Billard um halbzehn', in *Möglichkeiten des modernen deutschen Romans,* ed. Rolf Geissler. Frankfurt a.M. : Diesterweg 1962, p. 250.

27 From Hölderlin's poem 'Wie, wenn am Feiertag . . .' in the edition of Norbert von Hellingrath.

28 E.g. Karl August Horst: 'Überwindung der Zeit', in *Der Schriftsteller Heinrich Böll,* p. 67.

29 Just before eight o'clock Schnier has been in Bonn for almost two hours (p. 217); half an hour later he has still been there for only 'almost two hours' (p. 266). On the other hand Wilhelm Johannes Schwarz overlooks the fact that in *Haus ohne Hüter* both Frau Brielach and her daughter are called Wilma; his criticism here is groundless (*Der Erzähler Heinrich Böll. Seine Werke und seine Gestalten,* Berne/Munich : Francke 1967, p. 28).

30 *Frankfurter Allgemeine Zeitung,* 11.5.1963; reprinted in *Der Schriftsteller Heinrich Böll,* pp. 72-5.

31 To Werner Koch, printed in *Der Schriftsteller Heinrich Böll,* p. 102.

32 Arnold, pp. 38–9. Cf. *Labyrinth*, No. 6 (June 1962), pp. 3–4.

33 Op. cit., p. 324.

34 *Frankfurter Allgemeine Zeitung*, 28.7.1971. Also in *Der Schriftsteller Heinrich Böll*, p. 112.

35 *Die Zeit*, 6.8.1971.

36 *Merkur*, 25 (1971), p. 912.

37 Ibid., p. 914.

38 Michael Hamburger's translation.

39 A. Norman Jeffares, Introduction to W. B. Yeats: *Selected Poetry*, London: Macmillan 1962, p. xvii.

40 *Man sollte dagegen sein. Geschichten*, Olten/Freiburg i. Br.: Walter 1960, pp. 9–10.

41 *Der Sonderling in der deutschen Dichtung* (1943), 2nd edn, Munich: Hanser 1963.

42 Albert Camus: *L'Exil et le Royaume*, Paris: Gallimard 1957, p. 176. Cf. Theodore Ziolkowski: 'Albert Camus and Heinrich Böll', in *Modern Language Notes*, 77 (1962), pp. 282–91.

SELECT BIBLIOGRAPHY

Der Schriftsteller Heinrich Böll. Ein biographisch-bibliographischer Abriss, ed. Werner Lengning, offers in addition to a selection of articles on the writer an exhaustive list of works by and on Böll (but cf. my note 12). It is published by Deutscher Taschenbuch Verlag, Munich, and is updated at regular intervals. The latest edition appeared in April 1972.

Of the numerous interviews with Böll, the following are the most useful:

Horst Bienek: *Werkstattgespräche mit Schriftstellern*, Munich: Hanser 1962, pp. 138–51.

Im Gespräch: Heinrich Böll mit Heinz Ludwig Arnold, Munich: Boorberg 1971 (Edition Text + Kritik).

I WORKS BY BÖLL

Up to 1951 Böll's works were published by Middelhauve, Opladen, since then by Kiepenheuer & Witsch, Cologne.

Der Zug war pünktlich (1949)
Wanderer, kommst du nach Spa . . . (1950)
Die schwarzen Schafe (1951)
Wo warst du, Adam? (1951)
Und sagte kein einziges Wort (1953)
Haus ohne Hüter (1954)

Das Brot der frühen Jahre (1955)
Irisches Tagebuch (1957)
Doktor Murkes gesammeltes Schweigen und andere Satiren (1958)
Billard um halbzehn (1959)
Erzählungen, Hörspiele, Aufsätze (1961)
Ein Schluck Erde (1962)
Als der Krieg ausbrach. Als der Krieg zu Ende war (1962)
Ansichten eines Clowns (1963)
Hierzulande. Aufsätze zur Zeit (Munich: DTV) (1963)
Entfernung von der Truppe (1964)
Frankfurter Vorlesungen (1966)
Ende einer Dienstfahrt (1966)
Aufsätze, Kritiken, Reden (1967)
Hausfriedensbruch. Aussatz (1969)
Gruppenbild mit Dame (1971)
Gedichte (Berlin: Literarisches Colloquium) (1972)

II WORKS ON BÖLL

Albrecht Beckel: *Mensch, Gesellschaft, Kirche bei Heinrich Böll*, Osnabrück: Fromm 1966.

Hans Joachim Bernhard: *Die Romane Heinrich Bölls. Gesellschaftskritik und Gemeinschaftsutopie*, Berlin: Rütten & Loening 1970.

David Bronsen: 'Böll's women: patterns in male–female relationships', in *Monatshefte*, 57 (1965), pp. 291–300.

W. A. Coupe: 'Heinrich Böll's *Und sagte kein einziges Wort*—An Analysis', in *German Life and Letters*, 17 (1963–4), pp. 238–49.

Horst Haase: 'Charakter und Funktion der zentralen Symbolik in Heinrich Bölls Roman "Billard um halbzehn" ', in *Weimarer Beiträge*, 10 (1964), pp. 219–26.

Leopold Hoffmann: *Heinrich Böll. Einführung in Leben und Werk*, Luxemburg: St. Paulus 1965.

Klaus Jeziorkowski: *Rhythmus und Figur. Zur Technik der epischen Konstruktion in Heinrich Bölls 'Der Wegwerfer' und 'Billard um halbzehn'*, Bad Homburg: Gehlen 1968.

H. R. Klieneberger: 'Heinrich Böll in *Ansichten eines Clowns'*, in *German Life and Letters*, 19 (1965–66), pp. 34–9.

Enid Macpherson: *A Student's Guide to Böll*, London: Heinemann 1972.

Fritz Martini: 'Heinrich Böll: "Billard um halbzehn" ', in Moderna Språk, 55 (1961), pp. 27–38.

Therese Poser: 'Heinrich Böll: Billard um halbzehn', in *Möglichkeiten des modernen deutschen Romans*, ed. Rolf Geissler, Frankfurt a.M.: Diesterweg 1962.

Marcel Reich-Ranicki (Ed.): *In Sachen Böll. Ansichten und Aussichten*, Cologne: Kiepenheuer & Witsch 1968.

James H. Reid: 'Time in the Works of Heinrich Böll', in *Modern Language Review*, 62 (1967), pp. 476–85.

Wilhelm Johannes Schwarz: *Der Erzähler Heinrich Böll. Seine Werke und Gestalten*, Berne: Francke 1967.

Hermann Stresau: *Heinrich Böll*, Berlin: Literarisches Colloquium 1964.

Günter Wirth: *Heinrich Böll. Essayistische Studie über religiöse und gesellschaftliche Motive im Prosawerk des Dichters*, Cologne: Pahl-Rugenstein 1969.

W. E. Yuill: 'Heinrich Böll', in *Essays on Contemporary*

German Literature, ed. Brian Keith-Smith, London : Wolff 1966, pp. 141–58.

Theodore Ziolkowski : 'Albert Camus and Heinrich Böll', in *Modern Language Notes,* 77 (1962), pp. 282–91.

No. 33 of the literary periodical *Text + Kritik* (January 1972) is devoted to Heinrich Böll.

III   BÖLL IN ENGLISH TRANSLATION

The Train was on Time (*Der Zug war pünktlich*), tr. Richard Graves, London : Arco 1956 (repr. London : Sphere Books 1967).

Traveller, if you come to Spa (*Wanderer, kommst du nach Spa . . .*), tr. Mervyn Savill, London : Arco 1956.

Adam, where art thou? (*Wo warst du, Adam?*), tr. Mervyn Savill, London : Arco 1955.

Adam and The Train (*Wo warst du, Adam?* and *Der Zug war pünktlich*), tr. Leila Vennewitz, New York : McGraw-Hill 1970.

Children are Civilians too (stories from *Wanderer, kommst du nach Spa . . .*), tr. Leila Vennewitz, New York : McGraw-Hill 1970.

Acquainted with the Night (*Und sagte kein einziges Wort*), tr. Richard Graves, London : Hutchinson 1955 (repr. 1957).

The Unguarded House (*Haus ohne Hüter*), tr. Mervyn Savill, London : Arco 1957 (appeared as *Tomorrow and yesterday*, New York : Criterion Books 1957).

The Bread of our early Years (*Das Brot der frühen Jahre*), tr. Mervyn Savill, London : Arco 1957.

Irish Journal (*Irisches Tagebuch*), tr. Leila Vennewitz, New York : McGraw-Hill 1967 (repr. 1971).

94

Billiards at half-past nine (*Billard um halbzehn*), tr. Patrick Bowles, London: Weidenfeld & Nicolson 1961 (repr. London: Calder 1965).

Eighteen Stories (includes 13 stories from *Erzählungen Hörspiele Aufsätze* and four from *Doktor Murkes gesammeltes Schweigen,* also 'Warum ich kurze Prosa wie Jacob Maria Hermes und Heinrich Knecht schreibe'), tr. Leila Vennewitz, New York: McGraw-Hill 1966.

The Clown (*Ansichten eines Clowns*), tr. Leila Vennewitz, London: Weidenfeld & Nicolson 1965 (repr. London: Calder 1973).

Absent without Leave and other stories (includes *Entfernung von der Truppe, Als der Krieg ausbrach, Als der Krieg zu Ende war* and the *Eighteen Stories* mentioned above), tr. Leila Vennewitz, London: Weidenfeld & Nicolson 1967 (repr. London: Calder 1973).

The End of a Mission (*Ende einer Dienstfahrt*), tr. Leila Vennewitz, London: Weidenfeld & Nicolson 1968.

Group Portrait with Lady (*Gruppenbild mit Dame*), tr. Leila Vennewitz, London: Secker & Warburg 1973.